Trinidad & Tobago
Travel Guide

A Complete Guide on Exploring the Caribbean Jewel - Unveiling Cultural Delights, Pristine Beaches, Lush Landscapes, and Rich Heritage of Trinidad & Tobago

Juliet Bryan

Copyright © 2022 Juliet Bryan

All rights Reserved.

No part of this book may be reproduced, distributed, or transmitted in any form or by any means, including photocopying, recording, or other electronic or mechanical methods, without the prior written permission of the publisher, except in the case of brief quotations embodied in critical reviews and certain other noncommercial uses permitted by copyright law.

Dedication

This book is dedicated to those captivated by the vibrant spirit of Trinidad & Tobago. May it be your trusted companion, guiding you through remarkable journey in the Caribbean twin islands. Have fun!

Table of Contents

Chapter 1: Introduction to Trinidad & Tobago 1
    Introduction to Trinidad 2
    Overview of the Island 2
    History and Culture 3
    Geographical Features 4

Chapter 2: Planning Your Trip 9
    Best Time to Visit Trinidad 9
    Travel Requirements and Documentation 12
    Budgeting and Currency 15
    Packing Essentials 17

Chapter 3: Getting to Trinidad 21
    Flights to Trinidad 21

Chapter 4: Transportation Within Trinidad 26
    Public Transportation Options 26
    Driving in Trinidad 31
    Road Rules and Regulations 31
    Safety Tips 33

Chapter 5: Accommodation Options in Trinidad 35
    Hotels and Resorts 35
    Guesthouses and Bed & Breakfasts 40
    Vacation Rentals and Villas 45

Chapter 6: Exploring Trinidad's Attractions 52
    Port of Spain 52
    Northern Coast 58
    Eastern Coast 64
    Central Trinidad 69
    Southern Trinidad 73

Chapter 7: Introduction to Tobago 78
Exploring Tobago 78
    Getting to Tobago 78
    Transportation in Tobago 80
    Tobago's Top Attractions 82
Chapter 8: Trinidadian Cuisine and Dining 100
    Must-Try Local Dishes 100
    Popular Restaurants and Food Stalls 103
Chapter 9: Shopping in Trinidad 108
    Local Markets and Souvenirs 108
    Shopping Malls and Boutiques in Trinidad 115
Chapter 10: Outdoor Activities and Adventures 120
    Hiking and Nature Walks in Trinidad 120
    Water Sports and Diving in Trinidad 123
    Bird Watching and Wildlife Tours in Trinidad 128
Chapter 11: Traveling with Pets to Trinidad 132
    Research Pet Regulations and Requirements 132
    Pet-Friendly Accommodation 134
    Pet-Friendly Transportation within Trinidad 134
Chapter 12: Safety and Health Tips 136
    Emergency Contacts 136
    Health Precautions and Vaccinations 137
Chapter13: Cultural Etiquette and Tips for Travelers 141
    Respectful Behavior and Customs 141
    Understanding Local Traditions 143
Chapter 14: Language and Useful Phrases 147
    Official Language 147

Chapter 1: Introduction to Trinidad & Tobago

Welcome to Trinidad & Tobago Republic. The two twin islands just off the northeastern coast of Venezuela, in the southern Caribbean Sea. It is the southernmost island country in the Caribbean region. The larger of the two islands, Trinidad, is known for its lively culture, bustling cities, and diverse landscapes, ranging from lush rainforests to vibrant urban centers. Tobago, the smaller island, is celebrated for its tranquil beaches, coral reefs, and laid-back atmosphere.

The nation's cultural diversity is reflected in its music, dance, and cuisine, which blend African, Indian, European, and Indigenous influences. Trinidad and Tobago's annual Carnival is one of the most vibrant and colorful celebrations in the Caribbean, drawing tourists from around the world to partake in the festivities.

Tourists visiting Trinidad and Tobago can enjoy a wide range of activities, including snorkeling and diving in the clear waters, exploring nature reserves and bird-watching, and indulging in the flavors of the local cuisine. The islands are also home to a variety of wildlife, including the rare leatherback sea turtles that nest along their shores.

Trinidad and Tobago offer a captivating mix of natural beauty, cultural richness, and warm hospitality, making it a popular destination for travelers seeking both relaxation and adventure in the Caribbean.

Introduction to Trinidad

Trinidad, a vibrant island paradise located in the southern Caribbean. It is a land of rich cultural diversity, breathtaking landscapes, and warm hospitality. This tropical gem offers an array of experiences for travelers seeking a unique blend of natural wonders, historical heritage, and bustling urban life. From pristine beaches and lush rainforests to bustling cities and a melting pot of cultures, Trinidad is a destination that captivates the hearts of all who visit.

Overview of the Island

Trinidad, the larger of the two main islands that form the Republic of Trinidad and Tobago, is situated just off the northeastern coast of South America. It lies at approximately 10.5°N latitude and 61.5°W longitude, making it an ideal tropical escape with a warm and consistent climate throughout the year.

The island spans an area of around 4,768 square kilometers (1,841 square miles) and is home to a diverse population of approximately 1.4 million people. The majority of the inhabitants are of African, East Indian, and mixed-race descent, with smaller communities of European, Chinese, and Middle Eastern heritage. This cultural mix has significantly influenced the island's traditions, languages, and cuisine, creating a vibrant tapestry of customs and celebrations.

The capital and largest city of Trinidad is Port of Spain, which serves as the country's political, economic, and cultural center. The city's lively atmosphere is characterized by its colorful festivals, bustling markets, and historical landmarks, offering visitors a taste of the island's vibrant urban life.

History and Culture

Trinidad's history is a fascinating tale of conquest, colonization, and resilience, shaped by a series of cultural influences that have left a lasting impact on the island's identity. Before the arrival of European explorers, Trinidad was inhabited by indigenous peoples known as the Amerindians. The Arawaks and Caribs were the dominant tribes, and their presence is still evident in some of the island's place names and archaeological sites.

In 1498, Christopher Columbus arrived in Trinidad during his third voyage to the New World, claiming the island for Spain. However, it wasn't until the late 16th century that the Spanish began settling the island, primarily using it as a base for their South American expeditions. The island's fertile soil made it ideal for agriculture, and sugar cane plantations were established, leading to an influx of enslaved Africans to work the fields.

In the late 18th century, Britain gained control of Trinidad through the Treaty of Amiens. The British influence on the island was profound, as they continued the sugar plantation system and also brought indentured laborers from India to work on the estates after the abolition of slavery in the 19th century. This migration led to the emergence of a vibrant Indo-Trinidadian community, adding yet another layer of cultural richness to the island.

Today, Trinidad's cultural landscape is a fusion of African, Indian, European, Chinese, Middle Eastern, and indigenous influences. This diversity is celebrated throughout the year with colorful festivals, including Carnival, Diwali, Eid-ul-Fitr, and Chinese New Year. The island's music, dance, and culinary traditions also reflect this blend of cultures, making Trinidad a melting pot of artistic expression and culinary delights.

Geographical Features

Trinidad's geography is characterized by its varied terrain, which encompasses everything from sandy beaches and rolling hills to dense forests and mangrove swamps. The island's topography is a result of its volcanic origins and subsequent erosion processes.

The Northern Range, a series of low-lying mountains, stretches along the northern coast of the island. This range is covered in lush rainforests and is home to several stunning waterfalls, such as Maracas and Rincon Falls. The peaks of El Cerro del Aripo and El Tucuche offer breathtaking views of the surrounding landscape and the Caribbean Sea.

As you move southward, the land becomes flatter and is dotted with vast sugarcane fields and agricultural lands. The Caroni Swamp, a protected wetland area, is a significant feature of this region and serves as a habitat for various bird species, including the iconic Scarlet Ibis.

Trinidad's eastern and southern coasts are blessed with picturesque beaches and serene fishing villages. Popular destinations include Manzanilla, Mayaro, and Toco, where visitors can relax on the sandy shores, swim in the azure waters, and savor freshly caught seafood.

In contrast to the laid-back coastal regions, the western side of Trinidad is where the bustling city of Port of Spain is located. This cosmopolitan hub is a blend of modern skyscrapers, historical buildings, and lively markets. The Gulf of Paria separates Trinidad from its sister island, Tobago, which lies to the northeast.

Trinidad's climate is tropical, with a dry season typically running from January to May and a rainy season from June to December. The temperatures remain relatively consistent throughout the year, with the average ranging from 25°C to 32°C (77°F to 90°F), making it an enticing destination for those seeking warm, sunny weather.

As travelers venture into the heart of Trinidad, they will find a world of adventure, natural beauty, and cultural treasures waiting to be explored. The island's unique blend of history, culture, and geography creates an enchanting destination that leaves a lasting impression on all who set foot on its shores. Whether seeking relaxation on its pristine beaches, immersing in vibrant festivals, or trekking through lush rainforests, Trinidad promises an unforgettable experience for every traveler.

Beyond its lush rainforests and sandy beaches, Trinidad boasts a fascinating array of geographical features that make it a diverse and captivating destination.

The Pitch Lake

Located in the southwestern village of La Brea, Pitch Lake is one of Trinidad's most intriguing natural wonders. It is the largest natural asphalt lake in the world, covering an area of approximately 40 hectares (100 acres). The lake's surface appears solid, resembling a vast parking lot, but it is actually composed of thick, viscous asphalt. The Pitch Lake has been commercially mined for asphalt since the 19th century, and the material has been used for various purposes, including road construction and waterproofing.

Legend has it that the indigenous people of Trinidad used the asphalt from the Pitch Lake to caulk their canoes, leading to the discovery of this unique geological formation by Sir Walter Raleigh in 1595. Today, visitors can take guided tours to explore the lake's surface, learn about its geological significance and witness the natural phenomenon up close.

Nariva Swamp

The largest freshwater wetland in the nation is the Nariva Swamp, which is situated on Trinidad's eastern coast. This protected area encompasses over 60 square kilometers (23 square miles) and is a vital habitat for numerous plant and animal species. The swamp is fed by several rivers and waterways, creating a biodiverse ecosystem that includes mangroves, swamp forests, and marshlands.

The Nariva Swamp is a haven for birdwatchers and nature enthusiasts, as it provides a home to an impressive variety of bird species, including herons, egrets, ibises, and kingfishers. It is also an important nesting site for the endangered leatherback sea turtle, which comes ashore to lay its eggs during nesting season.

Visitors can explore the Nariva Swamp on guided tours, boat excursions, and nature walks, immersing themselves in the tranquility of this pristine natural environment.

Asa Wright Nature Centre

Nestled in the Northern Range, the Asa Wright Nature Centre is a renowned eco-tourism destination and birdwatcher's paradise. Established in 1967, this 270-acre estate provides a sanctuary for over 160 bird species, including the dazzling hummingbirds and the resplendent national bird, the Scarlet Ibis.

The center offers guided birdwatching tours, nature walks, and educational programs that provide insight into the rich biodiversity of the island. The verdant surroundings and scenic vistas make it an excellent spot for relaxation and bird photography.

Siparia Mud Volcanoes

Located in the southern part of Trinidad, the Siparia Mud Volcanoes are a unique geological feature that attracts both locals and visitors. These small, bubbling volcanoes erupt with a mixture of mud, water, and gas, creating an otherworldly landscape. The volcanic activity is relatively mild, and visitors can safely observe the mud pools from a distance.

Siparia is also a place of cultural significance, as it is the site of the annual La Divina Pastora Festival. Devotees from various religious backgrounds visit the mud volcanoes to pay homage to the statue of La Divina Pastora, the patron saint of the Roman Catholic Church in Siparia.

Gasparee Caves

Just off the northwest coast of Trinidad, accessible by boat, lie the Gasparee Caves. These limestone caves offer an exciting opportunity for exploration and adventure. The caves are adorned with stalactites and stalagmites, creating a surreal underground landscape. Guided tours allow visitors to traverse the cave's chambers and learn about their geological formation and historical significance.

The caves were once used by indigenous peoples and early settlers as hiding places and shelters during periods of conflict and adverse weather conditions. Today, the Gasparee Caves are a popular attraction for locals and tourists alike, providing a thrilling experience of subterranean exploration.

Trinidad's diverse geographical features, from natural asphalt lakes and mangrove swamps to lush rainforests and unique geological formations, offer an abundance of opportunities for outdoor enthusiasts and nature lovers. The island's commitment to preserving its natural heritage through protected areas and eco-tourism initiatives ensures that future generations can continue to enjoy the marvels of this captivating Caribbean gem.

Therefore, Trinidad's allure lies in its captivating blend of history, culture, and geography. From its cosmopolitan capital, Port of Spain, to its serene coastal towns and lush rainforests, the island offers a diverse range of experiences for every traveler. Whether exploring its rich history, indulging in cultural festivities, or immersing in the beauty of its natural landscapes, Trinidad promises an unforgettable journey filled with warmth, beauty, and hospitality. As visitors venture into this tropical paradise, they are sure to be captivated by its charms, leaving with cherished memories and a longing to return to this enchanting island.

Chapter 2: Planning Your Trip

When planning a trip to Trinidad, one of the most crucial factors to consider is the timing of your visit. The island's tropical climate and diverse range of events and activities throughout the year make it a year-round destination. However, understanding the weather patterns, cultural celebrations, and peak tourism seasons can help you make the most of your trip. In this guide, we will delve into the best time to visit Trinidad, taking into account weather conditions, local festivals, and travel considerations.

Best Time to Visit Trinidad

Trinidad's climate is characterized by warm temperatures and high humidity year-round, with two main seasons: the dry season and the rainy season. The best time to visit Trinidad largely depends on your preferences for weather, outdoor activities, and cultural experiences.

Dry Season (January to May)

The dry season in Trinidad typically spans from January to May. This period is considered the peak tourist season, as it offers the most favorable weather conditions for outdoor exploration and sightseeing. During the dry season, the island experiences less rainfall, lower humidity, and a higher chance of clear, sunny skies.

Weather

- Temperature: The average temperature during the dry season ranges from 24°C to 31°C (75°F to 88°F), providing a comfortable and warm climate for travelers.
- Rainfall: Rainfall is significantly reduced during this time, with occasional short showers or light drizzles. This makes it ideal for beach visits and outdoor activities.

Outdoor Activities

The dry season is perfect for engaging in various outdoor activities such as hiking, birdwatching, and exploring nature reserves. The cooler and drier weather makes trekking through the rainforests more enjoyable, and birdwatchers will have a better chance of spotting rare avian species in their natural habitats.

Beachgoers will also appreciate the calmer waters and clear skies during this time, making it an ideal period for snorkeling, diving, and relaxing on Trinidad's pristine beaches.

Cultural Events and Festivals

While the dry season is a popular time for tourists, it is relatively quiet in terms of major cultural festivals. However, visitors during February should not miss the world-famous Trinidad Carnival, which takes place in the weeks leading up to Ash Wednesday. Carnival is a vibrant celebration of music, dance, and colorful costumes, attracting revelers from all over the world.

Shoulder Season (June and November)

The shoulder seasons, which fall in June and November, offer a pleasant compromise between the dry and rainy seasons. These months are a great time to visit if you want to avoid crowds and still enjoy favorable weather conditions.

Weather

- June: The early part of June still experiences relatively dry weather, although there may be a slight increase in rainfall compared to the previous months.
- November: Similarly, early November tends to have drier conditions, but towards the end of the month, the rainfall begins to increase as the country transitions to the rainy season.

Outdoor Activities

During the shoulder season, outdoor activities can still be enjoyed, especially during the earlier part of June and November. The lush greenery and blooming vegetation after the rain showers create a picturesque setting for nature enthusiasts.

Cultural Events and Festivals

June is the month of Trinidad and Tobago's annual Corpus Christi celebrations, featuring vibrant street processions and religious ceremonies. It's an excellent opportunity to experience local customs and religious practices.

Rainy Season (June to November)

The rainy season in Trinidad spans from June to November, coinciding with the Atlantic hurricane season. During this time, the island experiences higher humidity levels and more frequent rainfall.

Weather

- Temperature: The average temperature remains relatively constant, ranging from 24°C to 31°C (75°F to 88°F).
- Rainfall: The rainy season brings heavier and more prolonged rainfall, often leading to localized flooding in certain areas.

Outdoor Activities

While the rainy season may deter some travelers, it can be a rewarding time for those who don't mind occasional showers and who appreciate lush green landscapes. Rainforests are at their most vibrant during this period, and waterfalls are in full flow, creating stunning natural vistas.

Cultural Events and Festivals

The rainy season offers several cultural events and festivals, including the Hindu festival of Divali (Diwali) and the Muslim celebration of Eid-ul-Fitr. Both festivals are marked by colorful displays, music, and cultural performances, offering visitors a chance to immerse themselves in Trinidad's rich religious diversity.

Travel Considerations

Hurricane Season

Travelers should be aware that the rainy season coincides with the Atlantic hurricane season, which runs from June to November. While Trinidad is generally less prone to direct hits from hurricanes compared to some neighboring islands, it's essential to monitor weather updates and be prepared for any potential disruptions.

Accommodation and Prices

The rainy season is considered the low tourist season, meaning there are fewer crowds, and accommodation prices may be more affordable. Travelers on a budget may find this period more appealing.

Travel Requirements and Documentation

Before embarking on your journey to Trinidad, it's essential to be well-informed about the travel requirements and documentation needed for a smooth and hassle-free trip. Trinidad has specific entry regulations that vary depending on your nationality, intended length of stay, and purpose of visit. This section will provide a comprehensive guide to the travel requirements and documentation necessary for traveling to Trinidad.

Passport and Visa Requirements

Passport

All foreign visitors must possess a valid passport with a minimum of six months validity from the date of entry into Trinidad. Ensure your passport is in good condition and has sufficient blank pages for entry and exit stamps.

Visa

Visa requirements for Trinidad vary depending on your country of citizenship. Some nationals may be visa-exempt, meaning they can enter Trinidad for tourism or short business trips without a visa. However, others may require visa, transit visa, or visa waiver. It's crucial to check the official website of the Trinidad and Tobago Ministry of National Security or consult the nearest Trinidadian embassy or consulate to determine the specific visa requirements for your nationality.

Visa Extensions

If you plan to stay in Trinidad for an extended period beyond your initial entry, you must apply for a visa extension at the Immigration Division of the Ministry of National Security. Ensure you submit the necessary documents and comply with any fees or additional requirements.

Entry and Exit Requirements

Departure Tax

There is a departure tax for travelers leaving Trinidad. This fee is part of your airline ticket cost. However, it's essential to double-check with your airline to confirm if the departure tax is included or if you need to pay it separately at the airport.

Return or Onward Ticket

Immigration authorities may require you to present a return or onward ticket as proof of your intent to leave Trinidad within the authorized stay period. Make sure to have a copy of your return flight or itinerary readily available when you arrive in Trinidad.

Yellow Fever Vaccination

Yellow Fever Certificate

If you are arriving in Trinidad from a country with a risk of yellow fever transmission, you will need to present a valid yellow fever vaccination certificate upon entry. This requirement is essential to prevent the spread of the disease and is particularly important if you plan to travel to other countries with yellow fever risk after leaving Trinidad.

Travel Insurance

Health Insurance

Although not a formal requirement, having travel insurance that includes medical coverage is highly recommended when traveling to Trinidad. Medical emergencies can happen at any time, and having adequate health coverage can provide peace of mind and financial protection in case of unforeseen circumstances.

Budgeting and Currency

Understanding the local currency and creating a budget for your trip to Trinidad is essential for managing your expenses and ensuring a comfortable stay. The official currency of Trinidad and Tobago is the Trinidad and Tobago Dollar (TTD), and the exchange rate may fluctuate, so it's beneficial to stay updated on current rates before your journey.

Currency Exchange

Banks and ATMs

Currency exchange services are available at local banks and ATMs throughout Trinidad. Banks typically offer competitive exchange rates, and ATMs are widely accessible in urban areas. Be mindful of potential transaction fees and inform your bank of your travel plans to avoid any issues with using your credit or debit cards abroad.

Currency Exchange Offices

Additionally, there are currency exchange offices located at the airport, major shopping areas, and tourist hubs, making it convenient to exchange your foreign currency for Trinidad and Tobago Dollars.

Cost of Living

Trinidad's cost of living can vary depending on your lifestyle and preferences. Generally, the country is considered moderately affordable for travelers, with opportunities to find both budget-friendly options and luxury experiences.

Accommodation

Accommodation costs will largely depend on the type of lodging you choose. Upscale hotels and resorts in popular tourist areas may have higher rates, while guesthouses, bed and breakfasts, and budget hotels offer more economical options.

Dining

Eating out can be affordable, especially if you explore local eateries, street food stalls, and food markets. Traditional Trinidadian dishes are flavorful and reasonably priced, offering a chance to savor the local cuisine without breaking the bank.

Transportation

Public transportation, such as buses and maxi taxis, is generally affordable and an excellent way to explore the island. Renting a car can be more expensive, but it provides greater flexibility for those looking to venture off the beaten path.

Activities and Attractions

Entrance fees to attractions and activities, such as nature reserves, historical sites, and cultural events, are typically reasonable. However, costs can vary depending on the specific experience and the level of guided services.

Tipping and Service Charges

Tipping is customary in Trinidad but not mandatory. Restaurants and hotels often add a service charge to the bill, so it's essential to check if a gratuity has already been included before leaving an additional tip. If a service charge is not included, leaving a tip of around 10% to 15% of the bill is considered a polite gesture for good service.

Budgeting Tips

- Research and Plan Ahead: Researching the cost of accommodation, activities, and dining options can help you create

a realistic budget for your trip. Having a rough estimate of daily expenses can assist in managing your finances while traveling.
- Travel Off-Season: Traveling during the shoulder or low season can result in lower prices for accommodation, flights, and activities. However, keep in mind that some attractions or services may have reduced operating hours during the off-season.
- Use Local Transportation: Public transportation is an economical way to get around Trinidad. Consider using buses or maxi taxis for short trips and save on transportation costs.
- Sample Local Cuisine: Exploring local eateries and food markets allows you to experience the authentic flavors of Trinidad without splurging on expensive restaurants.
- Souvenirs and Shopping: Set a budget for souvenirs and shopping to avoid overspending on memorabilia and gifts. Handmade crafts and local products can be wonderful souvenirs to bring back home.

Packing Essentials

Packing smartly for your trip to Trinidad ensures you have all the essentials for a comfortable and enjoyable experience. Here's a concise packing list to help you prepare for your journey:

Travel Documents

- Valid passport with at least six months validity from the date of entry into Trinidad
- Visa or visa waiver (if applicable)
- Yellow fever vaccination certificate (if applicable)
- Return or onward flight ticket
- Travel insurance documents, including policy information and contact details

- Copies of important travel documents (e.g., passport, visa, travel insurance) stored separately from the originals

Clothing

- Lightweight, breathable clothing suitable for tropical weather (e.g., t-shirts, shorts, dresses, skirts)
- Light long-sleeved shirts and pants for evenings and protection against mosquitoes
- suitable sandals or walking shoes for exploring
- Water-resistant footwear for rainy days and outdoor activities
- Swimwear for beach visits and water activities
- Hat or cap to protect from the sun
- Shawl or scarf for visiting religious sites and covering up during cultural events

Personal Essentials

- A small first-aid kit and prescription drugs
- Personal toiletries, including sunscreen (preferably reef-safe), insect repellent, and hand sanitizer
- Personal identification (e.g., driver's license, student ID, etc.)
- Prescription glasses, contact lenses, and a spare pair if applicable
- Reusable water bottle to stay hydrated

Electronics and Gadgets

- Camera or smartphone for capturing memories
- Electrical adapters and converters suitable for Trinidad's electrical outlets (Type A and B, 110V)
- Portable charger or power bank for keeping your devices charged on the go

Travel Accessories

- Lightweight daypack or beach bag for day trips and excursions
- Snorkeling gear
- Travel umbrella or compact travel blanket for picnics
- Travel lock for securing your luggage
- Waterproof pouch or dry bag for protecting electronics and valuables during water-based activities

Miscellaneous

- Cash in local currency (TTD) for small purchases and places that do not accept cards
- International credit or debit card with no foreign transaction fees
- Small notebook and pen for jotting down travel notes
- Reading material or entertainment (e.g., e-books, podcasts) for leisure time
- 2.4.7 Sun Safety:
- Sunscreen with high SPF to protect from the sun's rays
- Sunglasses with UV protection
- A wide-brimmed hat or cap for additional sun protection

Medications and Health Essentials

- Personal medications and prescriptions, along with a copy of the prescriptions
- Basic first-aid supplies (band-aids, antiseptic wipes, pain relievers, etc.)
- Over-the-counter remedies for common ailments (e.g., upset stomach, allergies)
- the use of insect repellent to keep off mosquitoes and other insects

consequently, by following the travel requirements and documentation guidelines, budgeting tips, and packing essentials outlined in this guide, you can confidently prepare for an enriching and enjoyable trip to Trinidad. With its tropical landscapes, vibrant culture, and warm hospitality, Trinidad promises an unforgettable adventure filled with treasured memories. Whether exploring its lush rainforests, participating in colorful festivals, or relaxing on its sun-kissed beaches, Trinidad welcomes you to experience the best it has to offer.

Chapter 3: Getting to Trinidad

As an enchanting Caribbean destination, Trinidad welcomes travelers from around the world seeking to experience its vibrant culture, stunning landscapes, and warm hospitality. Whether you're coming from nearby Caribbean islands, North America, Europe, or other continents, Trinidad is well-connected by air, making it easily accessible for visitors. In this comprehensive guide, we'll explore the various ways of getting to Trinidad, with a specific focus on flights to the island, including international flights and domestic connections.

Flights to Trinidad

Piarco International Airport (POS)

Piarco International Airport (POS) is the main gateway to Trinidad and Tobago and is located approximately 30 minutes from the capital, Port of Spain. It serves as the primary hub for international and domestic flights arriving in Trinidad. Piarco International Airport offers modern facilities, efficient customs and immigration procedures, and a range of services for travelers.

International Flights to Trinidad

Trinidad is well-connected to major cities in North America, Europe, and other parts of the world through direct and connecting flights. Several international airlines offer regular services to Piarco International Airport, making it relatively easy to find suitable flight options based on your departure location and travel preferences. Here are some key points to consider for international flights to Trinidad:

North America

From the United States

Various airlines, including American Airlines, Delta Air Lines, United Airlines, and JetBlue Airways, operate flights from several U.S. cities to Trinidad. Major departure points in the U.S. include Miami, New York (JFK and Newark), Fort Lauderdale, and Atlanta.

From Canada

Caribbean Airlines, WestJet, and Air Canada are some of the airlines offering direct flights from Toronto, Canada, to Trinidad. Other Canadian cities may have connecting flights to Trinidad through major North American hubs.

Europe

From the United Kingdom

Direct flights from London Gatwick to Trinidad are operated by British Airways. Additionally, there are connecting flights available from other European cities, such as Frankfurt and Amsterdam, through major international carriers.

South America and the Caribbean

From South America

There are direct flights from some South American cities, including Caracas (Venezuela), Panama City (Panama), and Sao Paulo (Brazil), to Trinidad. Caribbean Airlines, Copa Airlines, and Avianca are among the carriers that serve these routes.

From Other Caribbean Islands

Caribbean Airlines operates numerous inter-Caribbean flights connecting Trinidad to neighboring islands, such as Barbados, Jamaica, Antigua, and Grenada. These flights offer convenient options for travelers seeking to combine their Trinidad experience with visits to other Caribbean destinations.

Domestic Connections

If you're planning to visit Tobago or explore other parts of Trinidad, domestic flights and ferry services provide convenient travel options. Tobago, the smaller sister island of Trinidad, is accessible via regular flights from Piarco International Airport or by a scenic ferry ride.

Flights to Tobago

Trinidad and Tobago's domestic airline, Caribbean Airlines, operates frequent flights between Trinidad and Tobago. The flight duration is approximately 20-25 minutes, offering a quick and efficient means of island-hopping between the two destinations.

Ferry Services to Tobago

For travelers who prefer a leisurely journey with scenic views of the Caribbean Sea, the ferry service between Trinidad and Tobago is an excellent option. The Port of Spain Ferry Terminal, located in the capital, provides ferry services to the port of Scarborough in Tobago. The ferry ride takes about 2.5 hours and offers a chance to soak in the beauty of the surrounding waters and landscapes.

Airport Services and Immigration

Piarco International Airport provides a range of services and amenities for travelers, ensuring a smooth and comfortable arrival and departure experience. The airport offers duty-free shopping, dining options, car rental services, banking facilities, and lounges for both departing and arriving passengers.

Customs and Immigration

Upon arrival in Trinidad, passengers will proceed through immigration and customs clearance. Non-nationals will need to present their valid passports, visas (if required), and any necessary supporting documents, such as return tickets and proof of accommodation.

Travel Tips

Booking Flights

When planning your trip to Trinidad, it's advisable to book your flights well in advance, especially if you plan to visit during peak tourist seasons or major events such as Carnival. This will help you secure better fares and seat availability.

Visa and Documentation

Ensure that you have all the required travel documents, including a valid passport and any necessary visas, well before your departure date.

Travel Insurance

Consider purchasing travel insurance to provide coverage for unexpected situations, such as trip cancellations, medical emergencies, and lost baggage.

Check for Flight DealsKeep an eye out for airline promotions and flight deals, as airlines may offer discounted fares during certain periods or in conjunction with special events.

Flight Duration

Flight duration to Trinidad varies depending on the departure location. From North America, the flight duration can range from 3 to 5 hours, while flights from Europe can take approximately 8 to 11 hours, including layovers.

Chapter 4: Transportation Within Trinidad

Trinidad, with its diverse landscapes and vibrant culture, offers travelers an array of transportation options to explore the island's many attractions. From bustling cities to the serene countryside, navigating Trinidad is made easy through a well-developed transportation network. In this comprehensive guide, we'll explore the public transportation options available, including buses, taxis, maxi taxis, and car rental services, to help you make informed choices and enjoy a seamless travel experience within Trinidad.

Public Transportation Options

Public transportation in Trinidad provides an affordable and efficient way to get around the island. Whether you're traveling within the capital city of Port of Spain or exploring the countryside, these transportation options are readily available for both locals and tourists.

Buses

Buses are a common mode of public transportation in Trinidad, connecting various towns, cities, and neighborhoods. Operated by the Public Transport Service Corporation (PTSC), the bus system offers an extensive network that covers most areas of the island. Here's what you need to know about buses in Trinidad:

Types of Buses

The PTSC operates a fleet of buses, including standard buses and smaller mini-buses. Standard buses serve longer routes between major towns and cities, while mini-buses cover shorter distances and are often used for urban commuting.

Fares and Payment

Bus fares are typically affordable, making buses an economical option for travelers. Fares are paid in cash upon boarding the bus, and it's advisable to have small denominations of Trinidad and Tobago Dollars (TTD) for convenience.

Bus Stops and Routes

Buses follow designated routes, and their stops are marked with "Bus Stop" signs along the roadside. Route numbers are displayed on the front of the bus, indicating the destination and the major stops along the way. Timetables for bus routes can be found at PTSC bus terminals and online.

Frequency

Buses generally run at regular intervals during peak hours and less frequently during off-peak times. Peak hours are typically in the morning and late afternoon, coinciding with rush hour traffic.

Comfort and Amenities

Buses vary in comfort levels, with some being air-conditioned, while others rely on natural ventilation. Seating arrangements differ as well, with some buses having comfortable reclining seats, and others featuring bench-style seating. Additionally, some buses offer Wi-Fi connectivity for passengers.

Taxis

Taxis offer a convenient and flexible way to travel around Trinidad, providing door-to-door service for passengers. Taxis can be found at taxi stands, hotels, tourist attractions, and busy city areas. Here's what you need to know about taxis in Trinidad:

Types of Taxis

Taxis in Trinidad can vary in size and style. Traditional yellow taxis, similar to those in many other countries, are common in urban areas. In rural areas, you may find maxi taxis serving as shared taxis, offering a cost-effective option for short-distance travel.

Fares and Payment

Taxi fares are generally metered, and the rate is based on the distance traveled. Before setting out on a trip, it's wise to double-check the fare with the driver. Cash is the most common form of payment for taxi rides, and it's customary to tip the driver.

Taxi Stands

In urban areas, you'll find designated taxi stands where taxis wait for passengers. At these stands, you can easily hail a taxi or join a maxi taxi already en route to your destination.

Licensed Taxis

To ensure safety and reliability, it's advisable to use licensed taxis with visible license plates and official markings.

Comfort and Capacity

Taxi vehicles vary in size, but most can accommodate up to four passengers comfortably. Maxi taxis, on the other hand, are larger and can carry more passengers, typically up to 12.

Maxi Taxis

Maxi taxis are a unique form of public transportation in Trinidad, serving as a shared mode of transit between towns and cities. These large vans, typically brightly painted, provide an affordable option for traveling medium distances. Here's what you need to know about maxi taxis in Trinidad:

Shared Service

Maxi taxis operate on set routes, picking up and dropping off passengers along the way. Passengers share the vehicle with other travelers, creating a communal travel experience.

Fares and Payment

Maxi taxi fares are fixed based on the distance traveled. Payment is made in cash upon boarding the vehicle. It's advisable to have small denominations of TTD for payment.

Capacity

Maxi taxis can carry up to 12 passengers, including the driver. The seating arrangement may be bench-style or individual seats, depending on the model of the maxi taxi.

Designated Routes

Maxi taxis follow specific routes, and their destinations are indicated on the front or side of the vehicle. Popular maxi taxi routes connect major towns and cities across the island.

Maxi Taxi Stands

Maxi taxi stands are common at major transportation hubs, city centers, and busy areas. You can identify maxi taxi stands by the presence of multiple maxi taxis waiting to pick up passengers.

Car Rental Services

For travelers seeking greater flexibility and independence, car rental services are readily available in Trinidad. Renting a car allows you to explore the island at your own pace and access remote areas that may not be easily accessible by public transportation. Here's what you need to know about car rental services in Trinidad:

Rental Agencies

Numerous car rental agencies operate in Trinidad, including international companies and local providers. You can find rental offices at Piarco International Airport, major cities, and popular tourist destinations.

Rental Requirements

To rent a car, you must be at least 25 years old and possess a valid driver's license from your home country. Some rental agencies may have specific requirements or restrictions for younger drivers.

Rental Period

Car rental periods are flexible, with options for daily, weekly, or monthly rentals. Consider your travel itinerary and choose a rental period that best suits your needs.

Vehicle Selection

Car rental agencies offer a variety of vehicle options, from compact cars to SUVs. Choose a vehicle that accommodates your travel group and suits the terrain you plan to explore.

Driving in Trinidad

Traffic Rules

Driving is on the left side of the road in Trinidad, as in many Commonwealth countries. Observe local traffic rules, including speed limits and seat belt regulations.

Road Conditions

While major roads are generally well-maintained, some rural areas may have uneven or unpaved roads. Exercise caution and drive at a moderate speed on unfamiliar roads.

Navigation

GPS navigation or smartphone apps can be helpful for getting around Trinidad. Online maps are generally accurate, but it's always a good idea to have a paper map as a backup.

Road Rules and Regulations

Before embarking on your driving adventure in Trinidad, it's essential to familiarize yourself with the road rules and regulations to ensure a safe and stress-free journey. Here are some key points to keep in mind:

Driving Orientation

In Trinidad, as in many other Commonwealth countries, driving is on the left side of the road. The driver's seat is on the right side of the vehicle. If you're not accustomed to left-side driving, it may take some time to adjust, but with practice, it becomes more natural.

Driver's License

To drive in Trinidad, you must have a valid driver's license from your home country. If you plan to stay in Trinidad for an extended period, check whether your foreign driver's license is acceptable or if you need an International Driving Permit (IDP).

Minimum Age

The minimum age for driving in Trinidad is 25 years old. Younger drivers may face restrictions or need to pay additional fees when renting a car.

Seat Belts

Seat belts are mandatory for all passengers in the vehicle, including the driver. Ensure that everyone in the car is buckled up before starting your journey.

Speed Limits

Speed limits are signposted on roads, and it's crucial to adhere to them. In urban areas, the speed limit is typically 50 km/h (31 mph), while on highways, it may vary between 80 km/h (50 mph) to 100 km/h (62 mph).

Traffic Signals

Observe traffic signals, stop signs, and pedestrian crossings. Be prepared to stop at traffic lights and give way to pedestrians.

Drinking and Driving

The legal blood alcohol limit for driving in Trinidad is 0.08%. Driving under the influence of alcohol is strictly prohibited and can lead to severe penalties.

Mobile Phones

It is unlawful to use a mobile phone while driving unless you have a hands-free device. Avoid distractions and focus on the road to ensure your safety and that of others.

Child Safety

Children under the age of five must be securely strapped into an appropriate child restraint seat while traveling in a vehicle.

Safety Tips

Driving safety is paramount when exploring Trinidad. Here are some essential safety tips to keep in mind:

Defensive Driving

Practice defensive driving techniques, stay alert, and anticipate the actions of other drivers on the road.

Keep Left

Always keep to the left side of the road, and use your side mirrors to maintain awareness of traffic around you.

Avoid Night Driving

While driving during the day is generally safe, consider limiting night driving, especially in unfamiliar areas or rural regions where road conditions may be less predictable.

Seat Belts

Ensure that all passengers in the vehicle are wearing their seat belts at all times.

Emergency Kit

Carry a basic emergency kit in your vehicle, including a first-aid kit, flashlight, water, and some non-perishable snacks.

Animal Crossings

Be cautious of animals crossing the road, especially in rural areas.

Chapter 5: Accommodation Options in Trinidad

Trinidad, the vibrant and culturally diverse Caribbean island, welcomes travelers with a wide range of accommodation options that cater to different preferences and budgets. From luxury resorts to cozy boutique hotels, the island offers a plethora of choices for visitors seeking a comfortable and memorable stay. In this comprehensive guide, we'll explore the accommodation options available in Trinidad, with a particular focus on hotels and resorts. Whether you're looking for a beachfront escape, an urban oasis, or an eco-friendly retreat, Trinidad has something to suit every traveler's taste and needs.

Hotels and Resorts

Hotels in Trinidad are classified into different categories based on their amenities, services, and overall level of luxury. The categories typically range from budget and mid-range hotels to luxury and boutique hotels. Here's a breakdown of the different hotel categories in Trinidad:

Budget Hotels

Budget hotels offer affordable accommodations for travelers looking for basic amenities and a comfortable place to rest. These hotels often have simple rooms and limited facilities, and may be located in more modest neighborhoods. Budget hotels are an excellent choice for cost-conscious travelers who prioritize value for money.

Mid-Range Hotels

Mid-range hotels strike a balance between affordability and comfort. They typically offer more amenities than budget hotels, including on-site restaurants, Wi-Fi, and sometimes swimming pools. Mid-range hotels provide a higher level of comfort and service while still being reasonably priced.

Luxury Hotels

Luxury hotels in Trinidad offer top-notch facilities, exquisite design, and personalized services. Guests can expect spacious and elegantly furnished rooms, upscale dining options, spa facilities, fitness centers, and other premium amenities. These hotels often feature prime locations, such as beachfront or city center settings.

Boutique Hotels

Boutique hotels are characterized by their intimate atmosphere, unique design, and personalized service. They are often smaller in size compared to chain hotels and aim to create a distinct and memorable experience for guests. Boutique hotels in Trinidad may be located in charming colonial buildings, lush gardens, or exclusive beachfront settings.

Location Considerations

When choosing a hotel or resort in Trinidad, it's essential to consider the location that best aligns with your travel itinerary and preferences. The island offers various settings, each offering a different experience:

Port of Spain

As the capital city, Port of Spain is a bustling urban center with a mix of business, culture, and entertainment. Staying in Port of Spain provides easy access to restaurants, shopping, nightlife, and cultural attractions.

Beachfront

For a relaxing beach getaway, consider hotels and resorts located along the island's coastline. Popular beachfront areas include Maracas Bay, Las Cuevas, and Mayaro. These locations offer stunning ocean views and direct access to sandy shores.

Northern Range

The Northern Range is a lush and scenic region in Trinidad, popular among nature enthusiasts and hikers. Accommodation options in this area often blend seamlessly with the natural surroundings, offering a serene retreat.

East Coast

The east coast of Trinidad offers a quieter and more secluded experience, with stunning Atlantic Ocean views and unspoiled beaches. It's an ideal choice for travelers seeking a tranquil escape.

Hotel Amenities and Services

The range of amenities and services offered by hotels and resorts in Trinidad can vary based on their category and target audience. Below are some typical services and amenities that you can find:

Wi-Fi

Most hotels in Trinidad offer complimentary Wi-Fi access in rooms and common areas, keeping guests connected during their stay.

Restaurants and Bars

On-site dining options are available in many hotels, ranging from casual cafes to fine-dining restaurants. Some hotels also have bars or lounges for guests to unwind and enjoy drinks.

Swimming Pools

Many hotels feature swimming pools, providing a refreshing oasis for guests to cool off and relax.

Fitness Facilities

Luxury hotels and resorts often have well-equipped fitness centers, allowing guests to maintain their exercise routine while traveling.

Spa and Wellness

Some high-end hotels offer spa and wellness facilities, providing a range of treatments and therapies for relaxation and rejuvenation.

Concierge Services

The concierge desk can assist guests with travel arrangements, booking tours, and providing recommendations for local attractions and activities.

Business Facilities

Business travelers can find hotels with conference rooms, meeting spaces, and business centers, catering to their work-related needs.

Room Types

Hotel rooms come in various configurations, including standard rooms, suites, and executive rooms. Suites are often more spacious and may include additional living areas or private balconies.

Best Hotels and Resorts in Trinidad

Trinidad boasts an impressive selection of hotels and resorts that cater to different preferences and budgets. While preferences may vary, several accommodations consistently receive high praise from travelers for their exceptional service, facilities, and prime locations. Here are some of the best hotels and resorts in Trinidad:

Hyatt Regency Trinidad

Located in Port of Spain, the Hyatt Regency Trinidad offers a luxurious and contemporary experience. The hotel features stylish rooms, multiple restaurants, a rooftop pool, and a fitness center. It is conveniently situated near the city's business district and cultural attractions.

Hilton Trinidad & Conference Centre

Overlooking the capital city, the Hilton Trinidad & Conference Centre offers breathtaking views of the Gulf of Paria. The hotel features comfortable rooms, several dining options, a large outdoor pool, and a tennis court.

Magdalena Grand Beach & Golf Resort

Situated on Tobago Plantations Estate, this beachfront resort is a short distance from the airport and offers a picturesque setting with access to its own golf course. The resort boasts spacious rooms, a spa, multiple dining options, and a private beach.

Cara Suites Hotel and Conference Centre

Located in Claxton Bay, this hotel offers a relaxing escape with its beautiful garden setting. Guests can enjoy comfortable rooms, a swimming pool, and a restaurant overlooking the gardens.

Mount Irvine Bay Resort

Set on the western coast of Tobago, this resort offers a stunning beachfront location and access to a championship golf course. The resort features spacious rooms, a spa, multiple dining options, and a beachside pool.

Guesthouses and Bed & Breakfasts

For travelers seeking a more intimate and personalized experience during their stay in Trinidad, guesthouses and bed & breakfasts (B&Bs) offer a charming and welcoming alternative to larger hotels and resorts. These accommodations provide a homely ambiance, friendly hosts, and an opportunity to connect with the local culture and community. In this comprehensive guide, we'll explore the advantages and what to expect when choosing this type of lodging for your Caribbean getaway.

Advantages of Guesthouses and Bed & Breakfasts

Choosing to stay at a guesthouse or B&B offers several advantages for travelers, making it a popular choice for those seeking a more intimate and authentic experience:

Personalized Service

With fewer guests to cater to, the hosts at guesthouses and B&Bs can provide more personalized and attentive service. They are often happy to offer recommendations for local attractions, dining spots, and activities, ensuring guests make the most of their stay.

Cultural Immersion

Staying in a guesthouse or B&B allows travelers to interact with local hosts, providing an opportunity to learn about the culture, traditions, and way of life in Trinidad.

Homely Atmosphere

Guesthouses and B&Bs create a warm and homely atmosphere, making guests feel welcomed and comfortable during their stay.

Locally Sourced Meals

In many B&Bs, breakfasts are prepared using fresh and locally sourced ingredients, offering a taste of the region's culinary delights.

Community Connection

Guesthouses and B&Bs are often located in residential neighborhoods, offering a chance to connect with the local community and experience everyday life in Trinidad.

Unique Accommodations

Each guesthouse and B&B has its distinctive charm, with some offering picturesque views, traditional architecture, or garden settings that set them apart from standard hotel accommodations.

Locations of Guesthouses and Bed & Breakfasts

Guesthouses and B&Bs are scattered throughout Trinidad, offering a range of settings to suit different preferences:

Urban Areas

In cities like Port of Spain and San Fernando, you can find guesthouses and B&Bs tucked away in residential neighborhoods.

Despite being in the heart of urban centers, these accommodations provide a peaceful escape from the bustling streets.

Beachside Retreats

Along the coastline, especially in areas like Maracas Bay and Las Cuevas, you can find guesthouses and B&Bs offering picturesque views of the sea and direct access to sandy shores.

Nature Escapes

In the lush landscapes of the Northern Range or the serene countryside, guesthouses and B&Bs offer a retreat amidst nature's beauty. These accommodations are ideal for travelers seeking a peaceful and eco-friendly setting.

Historic Districts

In colonial towns like San Fernando and St. James, guesthouses and B&Bs may be found in charming heritage buildings, adding a touch of history to your stay.

Room Types and Amenities

Guesthouses and B&Bs offer a variety of room types, catering to different group sizes and budgets. The rooms may range from cozy single rooms to spacious suites, each adorned with unique decor and furnishings that reflect the hosts' personal touch. While the specific amenities vary depending on the establishment, here are some common features you can expect in guesthouses and B&Bs:

Cozy Bedrooms

Rooms are often designed to be comfortable and inviting, with cozy furnishings and thoughtful touches to make guests feel at home.

Ensuite Bathrooms

Many guesthouses and B&Bs offer ensuite bathrooms, providing guests with privacy and convenience.

Wi-Fi

Complimentary Wi-Fi is usually available for guests to stay connected during their stay.

Communal Spaces

Some guesthouses have communal areas, such as living rooms or garden spaces, where guests can relax, read, or socialize with other travelers.

Local Decor and Artwork

Guesthouses and B&Bs may feature local artwork and decor, showcasing the island's cultural heritage.

Breakfast

For B&Bs, a hearty and homemade breakfast is a standard offering, featuring local specialties and seasonal ingredients.

Garden or Terrace

Many guesthouses and B&Bs have outdoor spaces like gardens or terraces where guests can enjoy the island's natural beauty.

Laundry Facilities

Some accommodations may offer laundry facilities for guests' convenience.

Booking Considerations

When booking a guesthouse or B&B in Trinidad, consider the following factors to ensure a delightful and suitable stay:

- Reviews and Ratings: Read reviews from previous guests to gain insights into their experiences and the quality of service offered by the accommodation.
- Location: Consider the location in relation to your planned activities and attractions you wish to visit.
- Room Configuration: Check the available room types and configurations to ensure they meet your needs, especially if traveling with family or a group.
- Breakfast Options: For B&Bs, inquire about breakfast options and whether they can accommodate dietary preferences or restrictions.
- Special Requests: If you have any special requests or requirements, such as early check-in or dietary considerations, communicate them with the hosts in advance.
- Cancellation Policy: Familiarize yourself with the cancellation policy in case your travel plans change unexpectedly.

Recommended Guesthouses and Bed & Breakfasts

Trinidad offers a diverse selection of guesthouses and B&Bs, each with its own unique charm and offerings. While personal preferences may vary, the following are some recommended guesthouses and B&Bs that have garnered positive reviews and praise from travelers:

Kapok Hotel and Conference Center

Located in Port of Spain, this boutique hotel offers a combination of guesthouse-style charm and hotel amenities. It features comfortable rooms, a pool, garden spaces, and a restaurant serving local and international cuisine.

Salybia Nature Resort & Spa

Nestled in the natural beauty of the northeast coast, this eco-friendly resort offers guesthouses and cabins overlooking the Atlantic Ocean. It's an ideal retreat for nature lovers and those seeking a serene and secluded escape.

Le Grand Almandier

Situated in Mayaro, this beachfront guesthouse provides a tranquil setting along the eastern coast of Trinidad. It offers cozy rooms, beach access, and outdoor spaces to enjoy the sun and sea breeze.

L'Orchidée Boutique Hotel

Located in the San Juan area, this charming boutique hotel offers a mix of guesthouse-style intimacy and hotel comfort. It features beautifully decorated rooms, a courtyard garden, and a rooftop terrace.

Vacation Rentals and Villas

For travelers seeking a home-away-from-home experience and the freedom to create their own personalized vacation, vacation rentals and villas offer an excellent alternative to traditional hotels and resorts. Trinidad, with its vibrant culture, stunning landscapes, and warm hospitality, provides a diverse array of vacation rentals and villas to suit various preferences and group sizes. In this comprehensive guide, we'll delve into the world of vacation rentals and villas in Trinidad, highlighting their unique features, advantages, and essential considerations for a memorable and comfortable stay on this captivating Caribbean island.

Opting for a vacation rental or villa in Trinidad offers numerous advantages that cater to different travel preferences and group dynamics. Here are some key benefits of choosing these accommodations:

Privacy and Space

Vacation rentals and villas provide ample space for groups and families, allowing everyone to have their own bedrooms and common areas to socialize and relax.

Home-like Atmosphere

With fully equipped kitchens, living rooms, and dining areas, these accommodations offer a home-away-from-home ambiance, making guests feel comfortable and at ease.

Local Immersion

Staying in a residential neighborhood immerses travelers in the local culture and way of life, offering a more authentic experience of Trinidad.

Group and Family Travel

Vacation rentals and villas are ideal for group travel or family vacations, as they can accommodate multiple guests under one roof, making it easier to plan and coordinate activities.

Flexibility

Guests have the flexibility to cook their meals, follow their own schedules, and create a personalized travel experience.

Exclusive Amenities

Many villas come with additional amenities such as private pools, gardens, and outdoor spaces, providing an exclusive and luxurious experience.

Cost-Effective for Groups

Splitting the cost of a vacation rental or villa among several travelers can be cost-effective compared to booking multiple hotel rooms.

Locations of Vacation Rentals and Villas

Vacation rentals and villas can be found in various locations across Trinidad, catering to different preferences and interests. Here are some popular locations for these accommodations:

Beachfront

Along the island's coastline, from popular spots like Maracas Bay to secluded coves, vacation rentals and villas offer direct access to sandy shores and stunning ocean views.

Countryside

In the lush countryside and the Northern Range, you can find tranquil villas immersed in nature, providing a serene retreat amidst picturesque landscapes.

Urban Centers

Vacation rentals and apartments are available in urban centers like Port of Spain and San Fernando, providing easy access to city attractions, dining, and entertainment.

Residential Neighborhoods

Throughout Trinidad, vacation rentals and villas can be found in residential neighborhoods, offering an authentic experience of local life.

Types of Vacation Rentals and Villas

Vacation rentals and villas come in various types, ranging from cozy apartments to luxurious estates. Each type caters to different group sizes, preferences, and budgets. Here are some common types of vacation rentals and villas in Trinidad:

Apartments

Apartments are self-contained units within a larger building or complex. They are ideal for solo travelers or small groups and may offer basic amenities and kitchen facilities.

Townhouses

Townhouses are multi-story residences typically located in residential neighborhoods. They often provide more space and additional facilities, such as communal pools or gardens.

Beachfront Villas

Beachfront villas offer direct access to the beach and stunning views of the ocean. They often feature private pools, outdoor dining areas, and spacious living spaces.

Mountain Retreats

Villas nestled in the mountains or the Northern Range provide a serene escape surrounded by nature's beauty, making them perfect for nature enthusiasts and hikers.

Luxury Estates

Luxury villas and estates offer opulent accommodations with high-end amenities, such as private chefs, spa services, and expansive grounds.

Amenities and Features

The amenities and features offered in vacation rentals and villas vary depending on the property's size, location, and level of luxury. Here are some common amenities you can expect to find:

Fully Equipped Kitchen

Vacation rentals and villas typically come with fully equipped kitchens, allowing guests to prepare their meals and enjoy home-cooked dishes.

Private Pool

Many villas offer private swimming pools, providing a refreshing oasis for guests to relax and unwind.

Outdoor Spaces

Villas often have outdoor spaces like gardens, terraces, or balconies, providing opportunities for outdoor dining and relaxation.

Air Conditioning

Air conditioning is a standard feature in Trinidad's vacation rentals and villas, ensuring guests stay comfortable in the tropical climate.

Internet and Entertainment

Wi-Fi access, television, and entertainment systems are usually available for guests' convenience.

Laundry Facilities

Some properties may have laundry facilities, which are particularly useful for longer stays.

Housekeeping

Housekeeping services may be included, offering regular cleaning and maintenance during your stay.

Parking

Most vacation rentals and villas offer parking spaces, allowing guests to rent a car and explore the island at their leisure.

Booking Considerations

When booking a vacation rental or villa in Trinidad, consider the following factors to ensure a smooth and enjoyable experience:

Reviews and Ratings

Read reviews and ratings from previous guests to gain insights into the property's quality, amenities, and service.

Location

Consider the location in relation to your planned activities and attractions you wish to visit.

Group Size

Check the capacity of the property to ensure it comfortably accommodates your group.

Additional Costs

Inquire about any additional fees or charges beyond the rental price, such as security deposits or cleaning fees.

Special Requests

Communicate any special requests or requirements with the property owner or management.

Cancellation Policy

Familiarize yourself with the cancellation policy to understand the terms in case your travel plans change unexpectedly.

Recommended Vacation Rentals and Villas

Trinidad offers a diverse selection of vacation rentals and villas, each with its unique charm and amenities. While preferences may vary, the following are some recommended properties that have received positive reviews and praise from travelers:

Villa Being

Located in Tobago, this luxurious villa offers panoramic views of the ocean and lush landscapes. It features a private infinity pool, outdoor dining areas, and spacious living spaces with modern amenities.

Villa Sans-Souci

Situated on the picturesque north coast of Trinidad, this beachfront villa provides direct access to the sea and stunning sunset views. It offers a serene retreat with three bedrooms and a private pool.

Apex Villa

Nestled in the Northern Range, this eco-friendly villa offers a peaceful mountain escape surrounded by nature's beauty. It features a garden, terrace, and spacious living areas for relaxation.

Villa La Haye

Located in a residential neighborhood, this stylish townhouse provides a modern and comfortable setting with three bedrooms and a communal pool.

Villa Asaara

Situated on the western coast of Trinidad, this spacious beachfront villa offers a serene setting and direct access to the sea. It features a private pool, gazebo, and expansive outdoor spaces.

Chapter 6: Exploring Trinidad's Attractions

Port of Spain

Trinidad's capital city, Port of Spain, is a vibrant and culturally rich destination that offers a diverse array of attractions for visitors to explore. From historic landmarks to lush green spaces, the city provides a perfect blend of history, culture, and natural beauty. In this comprehensive guide, we'll delve into the top attractions in Port of Spain, including the iconic Magnificent Seven buildings, the expansive Queen's Park Savannah, and the serene Botanical Gardens, offering insights into their historical significance, cultural value, and what makes them must-visit destinations in Trinidad.

The Magnificent Seven

The Magnificent Seven is a collection of iconic and historic buildings located along Maraval Road and Queen's Park West in Port of Spain. These buildings showcase architectural splendor and represent different styles, reflecting the city's colonial past and diverse cultural influences. Each structure has its unique history and significance, making the Magnificent Seven a fascinating ensemble of buildings to explore.

Queen's Royal College (QRC)

Built-in 1904, Queen's Royal College is one of the oldest and most prestigious boys' schools in Trinidad and Tobago. Its architectural style is a mix of Romanesque and Spanish Renaissance influences, featuring striking arches, towers, and intricate detailing. The school has produced notable alumni, including prominent politicians, scholars, and artists.

Stollmeyer's Castle

This grand mansion, resembling a Scottish castle, was constructed in 1904 and was once the residence of a wealthy cocoa planter, Charles Fourier Stollmeyer. The castle showcases Scottish baronial architecture, complete with turrets, battlements, and a tower. Today, it is used for private events and functions.

Whitehall

Originally built in the 19th century as a private residence, Whitehall became the official residence of the Prime Minister of Trinidad and Tobago. This Neoclassical-style building features columns, verandas, and elegant interiors. It has played a significant role in the country's political history.

Hayes Court

Built in 1910, Hayes Court was once the residence of a wealthy businessman and is now the official residence of the Chief Justice of Trinidad and Tobago. The building boasts Edwardian-style architecture with ornate balconies and distinctive detailing.

Archbishop's House

This building serves as the residence of the Roman Catholic Archbishop of Port of Spain. It was constructed in the late 19th century and showcases Victorian architectural elements, including decorative fretwork and stained glass windows.

Roomor

Also known as Mille Fleurs, Roomor is a stunning French colonial mansion built in 1904. It was initially the home of a French count and later served as the residence of the French Ambassador to Trinidad and Tobago. The mansion's charming design includes wrought-iron balconies, verandas, and a tropical garden.

Ambard's House

Ambard's House, also known as Killarney, was built in 1904 and has a distinctive Palladian architectural style. It was constructed by a French architect for the prominent Ambard family. Today, the building serves as the residence of the Prime Minister of Trinidad and Tobago.

Visitors to the Magnificent Seven can appreciate the architectural beauty and historical significance of these landmark buildings, offering a glimpse into the city's colonial heritage and cultural diversity.

Queen's Park Savannah

Queen's Park Savannah is one of the most famous and significant landmarks in Port of Spain, encompassing 260 acres of vast open space in the heart of the city. Often referred to simply as "the Savannah" by locals, this historic park serves as a recreational and social hub, attracting visitors and residents alike for various activities and events.

Historical Significance

Originally a sugar plantation during the colonial era, the Savannah was converted into a public park in 1817. It was formerly known as the "Grand Parade" and served as a military training ground. Over the years, it has evolved into a beloved green space and a symbol of national identity for Trinidadians.

Key Features and Attractions

Open Green Space

The Queen's Park Savannah offers a large expanse of greenery, providing ample space for jogging, walking, picnics, and sports activities. The park's wide, circular perimeter road, known as "The Queen's Park Savannah Road," is popular among joggers and cyclists.

Picnic Areas

The park is dotted with shaded areas equipped with benches and tables, making it an ideal spot for picnics and family gatherings.

Festivals and Events

Queen's Park Savannah hosts numerous cultural festivals, concerts, and events throughout the year. One of the most notable events is the annual Carnival, where the park's Carnival bands gather to showcase their elaborate costumes and performances.

Emperor Valley Zoo

Adjacent to Queen's Park Savannah, the Emperor Valley Zoo is a popular family attraction, housing a diverse collection of animals from Trinidad and around the world.

Queen's Park Oval

Located within the Savannah, the Queen's Park Oval is a famous cricket stadium and a renowned venue for international and regional cricket matches.

Emperor Valley Mausoleum

Situated near the zoo, the Emperor Valley Mausoleum houses the remains of Sir Solomon Hochoy, a former Governor-General of Trinidad and Tobago.

Jogging Track

The Savannah's circular road offers a designated jogging track, making it a favorite spot for runners and fitness enthusiasts.

Botanical Gardens

The Royal Botanical Gardens, commonly known as the Botanical Gardens, is a serene oasis located in close proximity to Port of Spain's bustling city center. Spanning approximately 61 acres, these gardens offer a peaceful escape into nature, with a diverse collection of flora and fauna from both Trinidad and around the world.

Historical Significance

The Botanical Gardens were established in 1818 and are among the oldest of their kind in the Caribbean. They were originally created to cultivate and study economically important plants, such as spices and medicinal herbs. Over the years, the gardens have evolved into a recreational and educational attraction for both locals and tourists.

Key Features and Attractions

Tropical Plant Species

The Botanical Gardens boast an extensive collection of tropical plants, including exotic flowers, trees, shrubs, and orchids. The gardens are divided into various sections, each representing different plant species and ecosystems.

Orchid House

One of the highlights of the Botanical Gardens is the Orchid House, which houses a remarkable collection of vibrant and rare orchids from Trinidad and beyond.

Japanese Garden

The Japanese Garden is a tranquil and picturesque section of the Botanical Gardens, featuring traditional Japanese landscaping elements, a koi pond, and serene walkways.

The Avenue of Royal Palms

The entrance to the Botanical Gardens is marked by an impressive avenue lined with majestic Royal Palms, creating a grand and captivating entrance.

Birdwatching

The gardens provide an excellent opportunity for birdwatching, as various bird species can be spotted among the lush foliage.

Botanical Research

The Botanical Gardens also serve as a center for botanical research and conservation efforts, contributing to the understanding and preservation of Trinidad's plant biodiversity.

Educational Programs

The Botanical Gardens offer educational programs and guided tours for schools and visitors interested in learning about the diverse plant life of Trinidad and Tobago.

Relaxation and Recreation

The peaceful ambiance of the gardens makes it an ideal spot for relaxation, leisurely strolls, and enjoying a quiet escape from the city.

Northern Coast

The Northern Coast of Trinidad is a treasure trove of natural beauty, characterized by picturesque beaches, lush rainforests, and breathtaking landscapes. This region offers a diverse range of attractions for nature enthusiasts, adventure seekers, and those seeking a tranquil escape from the city's hustle and bustle. In this section, we will explore three must-visit destinations along the Northern Coast of Trinidad: Maracas Bay, Asa Wright Nature Centre, and Blanchisseuse.

Maracas Bay

Maracas Bay is undoubtedly one of the most popular and iconic beaches in Trinidad. Located on the northern coast, it is approximately 30 kilometers (about 19 miles) from Port of Spain, making it easily accessible for both locals and tourists. Maracas Bay is celebrated for its breathtaking scenic beauty, golden sandy shores, and the delicious local delicacy, "bake and shark."

Key Features and Activities at Maracas Bay

Pristine Beach

Maracas Bay boasts a stunning crescent-shaped beach with soft golden sand and clear turquoise waters. The beach is framed by lush green hills, creating a picturesque and tranquil setting.

Surfing and Bodyboarding

The waves at Maracas Bay are suitable for surfing and bodyboarding, attracting enthusiasts from near and far. Surfboard rentals are available for those looking to catch some waves.

Bake and Shark

One of the highlights of visiting Maracas Bay is indulging in the famous "bake and shark" sandwiches. This local delicacy consists of fried shark meat served in a "bake" (a type of bread) with a variety of toppings and sauces. Numerous food stalls line the beachfront, each offering its own unique twist on this savory treat.

Local Cuisine

In addition to bake and shark, visitors can also savor other delectable Trini dishes, including coconut water, doubles (a popular street food), and fresh seafood.

Picnicking and Relaxation

Maracas Bay is an excellent spot for picnics and beachside relaxation. Visitors can rent beach chairs and umbrellas to comfortably enjoy the sun and sea breeze.

Souvenir Shops

The beachfront area is dotted with souvenir shops where visitors can purchase local crafts, artwork, and beachwear as mementos of their trip.

Lush Hiking Trails

For nature enthusiasts and hikers, there are several trails that lead from Maracas Bay into the surrounding hills and rainforests, offering opportunities for exploration and birdwatching.

Visiting Maracas Bay

Maracas Bay is easily accessible by car or taxi from Port of Spain. The scenic drive along the Northern Range, with panoramic views of the Caribbean Sea and lush landscapes, adds to the overall experience.

There are also public buses that regularly ply the route from the city to Maracas Bay.

Best Times to Visit

Maracas Bay is a popular destination year-round, but it can get crowded on weekends and public holidays, especially during the Carnival season. For a more serene experience, consider visiting on weekdays.

Beach Safety

While Maracas Bay is generally safe for swimming, it's essential to exercise caution, especially during the rainy season when currents and wave conditions may change. Pay attention to any warning signs and follow the instructions of lifeguards.

Environmental Awareness

To preserve the pristine beauty of Maracas Bay, visitors are encouraged to practice responsible tourism by disposing of trash properly and respecting the natural environment.

Asa Wright Nature Centre

Asa Wright Nature Centre is a haven for nature lovers, located deep within the lush rainforests of the Northern Range. It is a private, nonprofit nature sanctuary and eco-lodge dedicated to conserving Trinidad and Tobago's biodiversity. The center's serene ambiance and rich biodiversity attract birdwatchers, nature photographers, and eco-tourists from around the world.

Key Features and Activities at Asa Wright Nature Centre

Birdwatching Paradise

Asa Wright Nature Centre is renowned for its exceptional birdwatching opportunities. The sanctuary is home to over 160 bird species, including toucans, hummingbirds, motmots, and the endangered Trinidad piping-guan.

Guided Nature Walks

Experienced naturalists lead guided nature walks through the rainforest, offering insights into the ecology, flora, and fauna of the region. The forest trails provide opportunities to spot various bird species, butterflies, and other wildlife.

Verandah Birdwatching

The center's main lodge features a large verandah where visitors can sit and observe birds and wildlife in their natural habitat. Bird feeders attract a constant stream of colorful visitors.

Natural Swimming Pools

The Asa Wright River flows through the sanctuary, creating natural swimming pools where visitors can take a refreshing dip.

Night Walks and Owl Watching

For a unique experience, the center offers night walks to observe nocturnal wildlife and owl-watching excursions.

Eco-Lodge Accommodations

Asa Wright Nature Centre offers eco-friendly accommodations with comfortable rooms and cottages nestled within the rainforest. Staying overnight allows guests to experience the serene ambiance of the rainforest after the 1.5 to 2 hours' driveday visitors have departed.

Environmental Education

The center hosts educational programs and workshops on environmental conservation, sustainable practices, and the importance of protecting Trinidad and Tobago's natural heritage.

Visiting Asa Wright Nature Centre

Asa Wright Nature Centre is located approximately 40 kilometers (about 25 miles) from Port of Spain, making it a feasible day trip or an overnight stay. The center operates on a reservation-only basis for guided tours and accommodations, so it's recommended to book in advance, especially during peak tourist seasons.

Accessibility

The trails within the sanctuary may involve uneven terrain and steep sections, so visitors should wear appropriate footwear and be prepared for moderate hiking.

Binoculars and Cameras

Birdwatchers and nature enthusiasts are encouraged to bring binoculars and cameras to capture the incredible biodiversity that the center has to offer.

Conservation Contribution

The entry fees and overnight stays at Asa Wright Nature Centre contribute to the conservation efforts and support the organization's initiatives in protecting the rainforest and its inhabitants.

Blanchisseuse

Blanchisseuse is a picturesque village nestled along the Northern Coast of Trinidad, known for its tranquil beaches, verdant rainforests, and refreshing rivers. It offers a quieter and more secluded experience compared to popular tourist destinations, making it an ideal spot for nature lovers and those seeking a peaceful retreat.

Key Features and Activities in Blanchisseuse:

Beaches and Scenic Coastline

Blanchisseuse is home to several beautiful beaches, each with its own unique charm. From the dark volcanic sands of Marianne Beach to the golden shores of Blanchisseuse Beach, visitors can enjoy the untouched beauty of Trinidad's northern coastline.

Paria Waterfall

One of the highlights of Blanchisseuse is the Paria Waterfall, a majestic cascade that tumbles over lush cliffs into a crystal-clear pool. The hike to Paria Waterfall is a popular adventure for hikers and nature enthusiasts, offering stunning views of the rainforest and the Caribbean Sea.

River Pools

Blanchisseuse is also known for its refreshing river pools, where visitors can take a dip in cool, clear waters surrounded by nature.

Hiking and Nature Walks

The surrounding rainforests and hills offer numerous trails for hiking and nature walks. These trails lead to hidden waterfalls, scenic viewpoints, and encounters with various wildlife.

Relaxation and Seclusion

Blanchisseuse provides a peaceful ambiance, making it an ideal destination for relaxation and unwinding amidst nature's splendor.

Visiting Blanchisseuse

Blanchisseuse is approximately a 1.5 to 2 hours drive from Port of Spain, depending on traffic and road conditions. The drive itself is a scenic journey through the Northern Range, offering glimpses of Trinidad's natural beauty.

Transportation

Accessing Blanchisseuse may require a private vehicle or organized transportation, as public transportation options are limited in this area.

Hiking to Paria Waterfall

The hike to Paria Waterfall typically takes about 2 to 3 hours each way, depending on the chosen trail and the pace of the hiker. It's advisable to embark on this journey with a guide or someone familiar with the route, as some parts of the trail can be challenging to navigate.

Conservation and Responsible Tourism

While enjoying the natural beauty of Blanchisseuse, it's crucial to practice responsible tourism and respect the environment. Avoid leaving litter behind, follow designated trails, and be mindful of wildlife and plants during your explorations.

Eastern Coast

The Eastern Coast of Trinidad is a coastal paradise that beckons travelers with its unspoiled beauty, pristine beaches, and laid-back charm. This region boasts some of the island's most stunning and secluded coastal destinations, offering a serene escape for beach lovers and nature enthusiasts. In this section, we will explore two must-visit beaches along the Eastern Coast of Trinidad: Manzanilla Beach and Mayaro Beach.

Manzanilla Beach

Manzanilla Beach is a hidden gem located on the northeastern coast of Trinidad. This stunning beach is renowned for its long stretches of golden sand, turquoise waters, and lush coconut palm trees lining the shore. With its tranquil ambiance and natural beauty, Manzanilla Beach is a favorite spot for locals seeking a peaceful retreat away from the city's hustle and bustle.

Key Features and Activities at Manzanilla Beach

Pristine Beach

Manzanilla Beach offers a long stretch of unspoiled coastline, perfect for leisurely walks, sunbathing, and enjoying the gentle ocean breeze.

Swimming and Water Activities

The calm and shallow waters at Manzanilla Beach make it an excellent location for swimming and wading. Families with children can safely enjoy the waters.

Beachcombing

The beach is a treasure trove for beachcombers, with seashells and coral fragments washed ashore.

Birdwatching

Manzanilla Beach is adjacent to the Nariva Swamp, a protected wetland area. As a result, the beach attracts a variety of bird species, making it a rewarding spot for birdwatchers.

Turtle Watching

Between March and August, Manzanilla Beach becomes a nesting site for leatherback turtles. Guided turtle-watching tours allow visitors to witness these majestic creatures as they come ashore to lay their eggs.

Picnicking and Camping

The spacious beachfront provides ample space for picnicking and setting up camp. Camping enthusiasts can obtain permits to camp on the beach for a memorable overnight experience.

Sunrise Views

Manzanilla Beach is renowned for its stunning sunrise views. Early risers can witness the sun majestically rising over the horizon, painting the sky with vibrant hues.

Visiting Manzanilla Beach

Manzanilla Beach is located approximately 60 kilometers (about 37 miles) from Port of Spain, which is about a 1.5 to 2-hour drive, depending on traffic and road conditions.

Accessibility

The drive to Manzanilla Beach takes visitors through picturesque countryside and coastal villages, offering glimpses of rural Trinidad's charm.

Turtle Watching Tours

To observe the nesting leatherback turtles, it's essential to join a guided tour with knowledgeable guides who will ensure minimal disturbance to the nesting process.

Beach Safety

While the waters at Manzanilla Beach are generally calm, it's essential to exercise caution, especially during the rainy season when currents and wave conditions may change.

Conservation and Responsible Tourism

As a protected nesting site for leatherback turtles, it's vital for visitors to adhere to guidelines and best practices during turtle-watching tours to ensure the preservation of these endangered creatures and their nesting habitats.

Mayaro Beach

Mayaro Beach is a tranquil and picturesque beach located on the southeastern coast of Trinidad. This idyllic stretch of coastline is known for its serene ambiance, gentle waves, and soft golden sand, making it an ideal destination for relaxation and beachside recreation.

Key Features and Activities at Mayaro Beach

Expansive Beachfront

Mayaro Beach spans approximately 12 kilometers (about 7.5 miles), providing ample space for beachgoers to find their perfect spot for sunbathing and picnicking.

Swimming and Water Sports

The waters at Mayaro Beach are generally calm and suitable for swimming, making it a family-friendly beach destination. Visitors can also enjoy water sports such as boogie boarding and beach volleyball.

Fishing

Mayaro Beach is a popular spot for fishing, and visitors may see local fishermen casting their lines into the sea.

Beachcombing

The beach is dotted with seashells and marine debris, making it an excellent spot for beachcombing and collecting souvenirs.

Seafood Delicacies

The surrounding area of Mayaro is known for its fishing industry, and visitors can enjoy delicious seafood dishes at local eateries.

Sunsets

Mayaro Beach offers breathtaking sunset views over the Caribbean Sea. Watching the sun dip below the horizon is a peaceful and awe-inspiring experience.

Visiting Mayaro Beach

Mayaro Beach is situated approximately 95 kilometers (about 59 miles) from Port of Spain, which is about a 2 to 2.5-hour drive, depending on traffic and road conditions.

Accessibility

The drive to Mayaro Beach takes visitors through charming coastal villages and scenic landscapes, offering a glimpse into the island's southeastern region.

Beach Safety

While the waters at Mayaro Beach are generally calm, it's essential to exercise caution, especially during the rainy season when conditions may change. Pay attention to any warning flags or signs indicating water safety.

Sun Protection

Given Trinidad's tropical climate, it's crucial to protect yourself from the sun while enjoying Mayaro Beach. Wear sunscreen, a hat, and sunglasses to shield yourself from the strong Caribbean sun.

Conservation and Responsible Tourism

As with all beach destinations, visitors are encouraged to practice responsible tourism by disposing of trash properly and respecting the natural environment.

Central Trinidad

Central Trinidad is a region of diverse landscapes and attractions, ranging from wetlands and bird sanctuaries to lush forests and adventure parks. This area offers a unique blend of natural beauty, outdoor activities, and opportunities to observe the island's rich biodiversity. In this section, we will explore two must-visit destinations in Central Trinidad: Caroni Bird Sanctuary and Chaguaramas National Park.

Caroni Bird Sanctuary

Caroni Bird Sanctuary, also known as the Caroni Swamp, is a wetland and protected area located in central Trinidad. This mangrove forest and swamp ecosystem provide critical habitat for various bird species, including the renowned national bird of Trinidad and Tobago, the Scarlet Ibis. Visiting the Caroni Bird Sanctuary offers a unique opportunity to witness spectacular bird gatherings and immerse yourself in the tranquility of nature.

Key Features and Activities at Caroni Bird Sanctuary

The Scarlet Ibis

The Scarlet Ibis, with its vibrant scarlet plumage, is one of the main attractions of the Caroni Bird Sanctuary. Visitors can witness these beautiful birds returning to their roosting site in the sanctuary during sunset, creating a stunning display of color against the evening sky.

Boat Tours

To explore the Caroni Bird Sanctuary, visitors can join guided boat tours that navigate through the narrow waterways of the mangrove forest. Knowledgeable guides provide insights into the diverse bird species and the delicate ecosystem.

Birdwatching

Birdwatchers will delight in the opportunity to spot a wide array of bird species, including herons, egrets, kingfishers, and many others that call the sanctuary their home.

Serene Nature Experience

The tranquil environment of the Caroni Bird Sanctuary offers a peaceful escape from the bustling urban centers. It is a place to connect with nature, listen to the sounds of the swamp, and observe wildlife in its natural habitat.

Flora and Fauna

Apart from birdlife, the sanctuary is also home to various reptiles, amphibians, and plant species, contributing to the rich biodiversity of the area.

Wildlife Photography

The stunning landscapes and abundant wildlife provide fantastic opportunities for nature photography.

Visiting Caroni Bird Sanctuary

Caroni Bird Sanctuary is located in central Trinidad, approximately 25 kilometers (about 16 miles) from Port of Spain, making it easily accessible for day trips.

Boat Tours

To fully experience the sanctuary, it's advisable to join one of the organized boat tours. These tours usually depart in the late afternoon to witness the Scarlet Ibis returning to their roosts at sunset.

Guided Tours

Local tour operators and guides offer guided tours of the sanctuary, ensuring an informative and enriching experience for visitors.

Sunset Timing

The best time to witness the Scarlet Ibis spectacle is during the late afternoon, just before sunset. It's essential to check with tour operators for the exact timing of the boat tours, as the Scarlet Ibis returns to the swamp at different times depending on the season.

Conservation Efforts

Caroni Bird Sanctuary is a protected area, and visitors are encouraged to respect the sanctuary's rules and guidelines to preserve its delicate ecosystem and wildlife.

Chaguaramas National Park

Chaguaramas National Park is a vast natural area located on the northwestern peninsula of Trinidad. This diverse park encompasses dense forests, rugged hills, secluded beaches, and historical landmarks. It is a haven for outdoor enthusiasts, history buffs, and nature lovers alike, offering an array of activities and attractions.

Key Features and Activities at Chaguaramas National Park

Hiking and Nature Trails

Chaguaramas National Park features numerous hiking and nature trails that lead to scenic viewpoints, hidden coves, and historical sites.

The trails cater to different skill levels, providing opportunities for leisurely walks and more challenging hikes.

Macqueripe Beach

Macqueripe Beach is a secluded bay with calm waters, making it ideal for swimming and snorkeling. The beach is surrounded by cliffs and lush greenery, adding to its picturesque beauty.

Kayaking and Paddleboarding

The calm waters of Chaguaramas Bay provide an excellent setting for kayaking and paddleboarding, allowing visitors to explore the coastline and observe marine life.

Zip Lining

For adrenaline seekers, the Chaguaramas National Park offers a thrilling zip-lining adventure that takes participants through the treetops, offering stunning aerial views of the park.

Historical Sites

The park is home to several historical sites, including the military museum at Fort George, the World War II-era Tucker Valley Radar Station, and the historic Signal Hill Battery.

Chacachacare Island

Located just off the coast of Chaguaramas, Chacachacare Island is accessible by boat and offers a fascinating glimpse into Trinidad's history, with its abandoned leper colony and old lighthouse.

Wildlife Observation

Chaguaramas National Park is home to a variety of wildlife, including various bird species, iguanas, and butterflies, making it a rewarding destination for wildlife observation and photography.

Visiting Chaguaramas National Park

Chaguaramas National Park is easily accessible from Port of Spain and other nearby areas by car or taxi.

Entry Fees

There may be nominal entry fees for accessing specific areas or participating in certain activities within the park. It's advisable to check the current fees and operating hours before visiting.

Hiking

When embarking on hikes or nature walks in the park, it's essential to wear appropriate footwear, carry sufficient water, and be mindful of the terrain.

Beach Safety

While the beaches in Chaguaramas National Park are generally safe for swimming, it's essential to exercise caution, especially during the rainy season when conditions may change.

Conservation and Responsible Tourism

As with all natural areas, visitors are encouraged to practice responsible tourism by disposing of trash properly and respecting the environment.

Southern Trinidad

Southern Trinidad is a region characterized by its unique geological formations, cultural landmarks, and historical significance. From the world's largest natural asphalt lake to picturesque viewpoints offering panoramic vistas, the attractions in Southern Trinidad offer a diverse range of experiences for travelers. In this section, we will explore two must-visit destinations in Southern Trinidad: Pitch Lake in La Brea and San Fernando Hill.

Pitch Lake in La Brea

Pitch Lake in La Brea is a fascinating natural wonder and one of Trinidad's most unique attractions. It is the world's largest natural deposit of asphalt, covering an area of approximately 40 hectares (about 98 acres). This remarkable phenomenon has been attracting visitors for centuries and continues to intrigue scientists and tourists alike.

Key Features and Activities at Pitch Lake

Unique Geological Formation

Pitch Lake formed millions of years ago when the Caribbean tectonic plate collided with the South American plate. This collision caused oil and gas to be forced to the surface, and over time, the lighter elements evaporated, leaving behind the dense asphalt lake.

Exploration of the Lake

Visitors can take guided tours to explore the surface of Pitch Lake. The lake's surface is solid enough to walk on, and visitors can observe the bubbling bitumen, tar pits, and interesting geological formations.

Natural Medicinal Properties

The asphalt of Pitch Lake is believed to have natural healing properties. Some visitors indulge in a unique experience called "pitch bathing," where they immerse themselves in the warm asphalt, which is said to have therapeutic benefits for various skin conditions.

Historical Significance

Pitch Lake has been commercially exploited since the 19th century, with the asphalt used in the construction of roads and buildings around the world. The lake's economic significance is deeply rooted in Trinidad's history.

Visitor Center

The Pitch Lake Visitor Center provides information about the history, geology, and significance of the lake. It also offers educational exhibits and displays related to the asphalt industry.

Visiting Pitch Lake

Pitch Lake is located in La Brea, approximately 70 kilometers (about 43 miles) from Port of Spain, which is about a 1.5 to 2-hour drive, depending on traffic and road conditions.

Guided Tours

Visitors must join guided tours to explore Pitch Lake safely. The knowledgeable guides provide insights into the geological formation, historical significance, and unique features of the lake.

Appropriate Attire

When visiting Pitch Lake, it's essential to wear comfortable footwear suitable for walking on the asphalt surface. Additionally, wearing long pants and closed-toe shoes is advisable to protect against sticky asphalt.

Conservation and Preservation

Pitch Lake is a natural wonder and a critical geological site, and visitors are encouraged to respect the area and refrain from causing any damage to the surface.

San Fernando Hill

San Fernando Hill is a prominent landmark located in the city of San Fernando, the second-largest city in Trinidad and Tobago. Rising 192 meters (about 630 feet) above sea level, this hill offers panoramic views of the southern landscape, the Gulf of Paria, and even the northern mountain ranges on clear days. It is a popular spot for locals and tourists alike to enjoy breathtaking vistas and appreciate the natural beauty of Southern Trinidad.

Key Features and Activities at San Fernando Hill

Viewpoints and Observation Decks

San Fernando Hill features well-maintained viewpoints and observation decks that offer sweeping views of the city of San Fernando, the Gulf of Paria, and the surrounding landscape. The panorama is particularly enchanting during sunrise and sunset.

Hiking and Nature Walks

The hill is accessible via a paved road that winds through lush greenery. Hiking to the summit provides a refreshing and enjoyable experience for nature enthusiasts.

Picnicking and Recreation

San Fernando Hill offers ample space for picnicking and leisure activities. Families and groups often gather to enjoy quality time amidst the natural beauty of the hilltop.

Historical Significance

The hill has historical significance as it was the site of an important signal station during the 19th century, used for communication and surveillance purposes.

Peaceful Retreat

San Fernando Hill provides a peaceful and serene setting, allowing visitors to escape the urban buzz and connect with nature.

Visiting San Fernando Hill

San Fernando Hill is located in the city of San Fernando, which is approximately 35 kilometers (about 22 miles) from Port of Spain, making it accessible by car or public transportation.

Hiking to the Summit

The hike to the summit of San Fernando Hill is relatively easy and suitable for individuals of all ages and fitness levels. The paved road and steps make the ascent comfortable and safe.

Sunrise and Sunset

The best times to visit San Fernando Hill are during sunrise and sunset, as the changing colors of the sky paint a stunning backdrop to the surrounding landscape.

Conservation and Responsible Tourism

Visitors are encouraged to respect the natural environment of San Fernando Hill and refrain from littering or causing any damage to the area.

Chapter 7: Introduction to Tobago

Exploring Tobago

Tobago, the smaller sister island of Trinidad, is a paradise of natural beauty, pristine beaches, lush rainforests, and vibrant coral reefs. This Caribbean gem offers a more laid-back and tranquil experience compared to its bustling counterpart, Trinidad. Tobago's attractions range from stunning coastal landscapes and waterfalls to historical landmarks and unique wildlife encounters. In this section, we will explore the must-visit attractions of Tobago, each offering a unique and unforgettable experience for travelers.

Getting to Tobago

Tobago, the smaller of the two main islands that make up the twin-island nation of Trinidad and Tobago, is a tropical paradise known for its pristine beaches, lush rainforests, and vibrant coral reefs. Travelers from all over the world are drawn to Tobago's natural beauty and laid-back charm. While Tobago is a separate island, getting there is relatively easy, with several transportation options available. In this section, we will explore the different ways of getting to Tobago and the logistics involved.

By Air

The most common and convenient way to get to Tobago is by air. Tobago has its own international airport, the Arthur Napoleon Raymond Robinson International Airport, commonly known as Crown Point Airport (TAB). This airport is the main gateway for both domestic and international flights to Tobago.

International Flights to Tobago

Several international airlines operate direct flights to Tobago from major cities in North America, Europe, and other Caribbean islands. Some of the airlines that offer international flights to Tobago include Caribbean Airlines, British Airways, and Condor Airlines.

Domestic Flights from Trinidad to Tobago

If you are already in Trinidad, you can easily catch a domestic flight to Tobago. The flight from Piarco International Airport (POS) in Trinidad to Crown Point Airport (TAB) in Tobago takes approximately 20 to 25 minutes.

Airport Transfer

Upon arriving at Crown Point Airport in Tobago, travelers can easily find taxis and rental car services available at the airport to take them to their accommodations.

By Ferry

Another option for getting to Tobago is by ferry. There are regular ferry services that operate between Trinidad and Tobago, providing a scenic and budget-friendly transportation option.

Port of Spain to Scarborough Ferry

The ferry route connects the capital city of Trinidad, Port of Spain, to Scarborough, Tobago's main town. The ferry ride takes approximately 2.5 to 3 hours, offering travelers the chance to enjoy picturesque views of the Caribbean Sea.

Ferry Schedule and Ticketing

The ferry schedule may vary, so it's essential to check the departure times in advance and purchase tickets early, especially during peak travel seasons and holidays. Tickets can be purchased at the Port of Spain ferry terminal or online through the Trinidad and Tobago Inter-Island Transportation Company (TTIT) website.

Facilities on the Ferry

The ferry is equipped with comfortable seating, restrooms, and a snack bar where passengers can purchase food and beverages.

Transportation in Tobago

Upon arriving in Scarborough, Tobago, travelers can find taxis and rental car services available at the port to take them to their accommodations or explore the island.

Private Yachts and Sailboats

For travelers who enjoy sailing, Tobago is also accessible by private yachts and sailboats. Tobago has several marinas and docking facilities where private boats can anchor.

Customs and Immigration

Before arriving in Tobago, private boat owners and their passengers must clear customs and immigration formalities at the designated port of entry. It is essential to have all necessary travel documents and comply with immigration regulations.

Island Hopping in the Caribbean

Tobago is a popular destination for those sailing around the Caribbean islands. Travelers can enjoy island hopping experiences and explore the unique beauty of each island in the region.

Helicopter Charter

For a luxurious and scenic mode of transportation, some private helicopter charter companies offer services between Trinidad and Tobago. Helicopter charters provide a swift and picturesque journey, allowing passengers to enjoy breathtaking aerial views of the islands.

Charter Booking

Private helicopter charters must be booked in advance with the charter company, and passengers should inquire about luggage restrictions and other important details.

Scenic Aerial Tours

In addition to transportation between the islands, helicopter charters also offer scenic aerial tours of Tobago, providing an unforgettable perspective of the island's natural beauty.

Travel Tips for Getting to Tobago

Travel Documents: Ensure that you have all the necessary travel documents, including a valid passport and any required visas, before traveling to Tobago.

Flight and Ferry Reservations

Book your flights or ferry tickets well in advance, especially during peak travel seasons and holidays, to secure your preferred travel dates and times.

Airport Transfers

If arriving by air, consider arranging airport transfers in advance to ensure a smooth and hassle-free journey to your accommodations.
Ferry Schedules: Check the ferry schedules and plan your trip accordingly to avoid any inconveniences or delays.

Luggage Restrictions

Be aware of luggage restrictions and regulations for both flights and ferry travel to avoid any issues during check-in or boarding.

Travel Insurance

Consider purchasing travel insurance to protect yourself against unexpected circumstances or travel disruptions.

Cash and Currency

While there are ATMs and currency exchange services available, it's a good idea to have some local currency (Trinidad and Tobago dollars) on hand for small expenses or emergencies.
Exploring Trinidad's Attractions:

Tobago's Top Attractions

Tobago, the smaller sister island of Trinidad, is a tropical paradise known for its stunning natural beauty, crystal-clear waters, lush rainforests, and vibrant marine life. The island offers a diverse range of attractions and activities for travelers seeking both relaxation and adventure. From pristine beaches and captivating waterfalls to vibrant coral reefs and historical landmarks, Tobago's top attractions showcase the island's unique charm and cultural heritage. In this section, we will explore Tobago's top attractions, each offering a memorable and enriching experience for visitors.

Pigeon Point Beach

Pigeon Point Beach is Tobago's most famous and iconic beach, often referred to as the "Crown Jewel of Tobago." This postcard-perfect beach is renowned for its powdery white sand, turquoise waters, and swaying coconut palm trees, creating a picture-perfect tropical paradise.

Key Features and Activities at Pigeon Point Beach

Beach Relaxation

Pigeon Point Beach is the ideal spot for beach lovers to relax, sunbathe, and soak up the Caribbean sun. The gentle sea breeze and warm waters make it a soothing and inviting environment.

Water Sports

The calm and shallow waters of Pigeon Point Beach are perfect for water sports activities such as snorkeling, paddleboarding, kayaking, and windsurfing. The abundant marine life and colorful coral reefs make it a favorite spot for underwater exploration.

Nylon Pool

A short boat ride from Pigeon Point Beach takes visitors to the famous Nylon Pool, a shallow sandbar with crystal-clear waters, resembling a swimming pool in the middle of the sea. It is a popular spot for swimming and enjoying the serene environment.

Beach Facilities

Pigeon Point Beach is well-equipped with amenities such as restrooms, changing facilities, beach chairs, and umbrellas, ensuring visitors have a comfortable beach experience.

Local Cuisine

The beach is surrounded by vendors and beach bars offering delicious local dishes, refreshing tropical drinks, and fresh coconut water.

Visiting Pigeon Point Beach

Pigeon Point Beach is located on the southwestern tip of Tobago, near Crown Point. It is easily accessible by car, taxi, or public transportation from various parts of the island.

Entrance Fee

There is an entrance fee to access Pigeon Point Beach, which contributes to the maintenance and preservation of the area.

Boat Tours to Nylon Pool

Boat tours to Nylon Pool can be arranged at Pigeon Point Beach. The tours usually include stops at Buccoo Reef for snorkeling and exploring the vibrant marine life.

Argyle Waterfall

Argyle Waterfall is a majestic three-tiered cascade nestled within the lush rainforests of Tobago's interior. It is one of the island's most famous waterfalls and a popular destination for nature enthusiasts and hikers.

Key Features and Activities at Argyle Waterfall

Hiking and Nature Walks

The hike to Argyle Waterfall takes visitors through a scenic trail within the rainforest, providing opportunities to spot various plant and animal species along the way. The journey is refreshing and rewarding, making it a favorite among nature enthusiasts and photographers.

Swimming

The base of the waterfall offers a natural pool where visitors can take a refreshing dip in the cool, clear waters, surrounded by the beauty of nature. Swimming beneath the cascading waters is a memorable and invigorating experience.

Photography

The breathtaking beauty of Argyle Waterfall makes it an ideal spot for photography. The lush greenery, cascading waters, and natural rock formations provide stunning photo opportunities.

Birdwatching

The rainforest surrounding Argyle Waterfall is home to an array of bird species, making it a rewarding location for birdwatching enthusiasts.

Visiting Argyle Waterfall

Argyle Waterfall is situated in the village of Roxborough in Tobago's eastern region. It is approximately 32 kilometers (about 20 miles) from Scarborough, the island's capital, and the journey takes approximately 45 minutes by car or taxi.

Hiking Difficulty

The hike to Argyle Waterfall is considered moderately challenging. It is recommended to wear comfortable hiking shoes and bring insect repellent for a more enjoyable experience.

Safety Precautions

While swimming is allowed at the waterfall's base, it's essential to exercise caution, especially during rainy periods when water levels may rise.

Buccoo Reef and Nylon Pool

Buccoo Reef is a vibrant coral reef located just off the southwestern coast of Tobago. It is one of the most accessible coral reefs in the Caribbean and offers fantastic opportunities for snorkeling and underwater exploration. The nearby Nylon Pool is a shallow sandbar with clear waters, creating an experience similar to swimming in a natural pool.

Key Features and Activities at Buccoo Reef and Nylon Pool

Glass Bottom Boat Tours

Visitors can take glass bottom boat tours to Buccoo Reef, allowing them to observe the colorful marine life and coral formations without getting wet. Knowledgeable guides provide insights into the underwater world and its delicate ecosystem.

Snorkeling

For a closer encounter with marine life, snorkeling at Buccoo Reef offers an immersive experience, with opportunities to see vibrant fish, corals, and even small stingrays.

Nylon Pool Experience

After exploring Buccoo Reef, visitors can head to the nearby Nylon Pool for a unique swimming experience in the middle of the sea. The calm and shallow waters of Nylon Pool create a serene and safe environment for swimming and relaxing.

Coral Gardens

Coral Gardens, located adjacent to Buccoo Reef, is another popular snorkeling spot known for its beautiful coral formations and diverse marine species.

Visiting Buccoo Reef and Nylon Pool

Buccoo Reef and Nylon Pool are located on Tobago's southwestern coast, and visitors can access these attractions through organized boat tours from various locations, including Pigeon Point and Store Bay.

Glass Bottom Boat Tours

Several tour operators offer glass bottom boat tours to Buccoo Reef and Nylon Pool. These tours typically include snorkeling gear for visitors to explore the underwater world.

Swimming at Nylon Pool

The shallow waters of Nylon Pool create a serene and safe environment for swimming, making it a popular spot for both adults and children.

Marine Conservation

While exploring Buccoo Reef, it's essential to practice responsible snorkeling by avoiding touching or damaging the coral reefs, as they are fragile and vital to marine ecosystems.

Fort King George

Fort King George is a historical site and a well-preserved fortification dating back to the 18th century. Located on a hilltop overlooking Scarborough, Tobago's capital, this fort offers not only historical significance but also stunning views of the town and the surrounding coastline.

Key Features and Activities at Fort King George

Historical Tour

Fort King George houses a museum that offers insight into Tobago's colonial history, with exhibits showcasing artifacts and information about the island's past. Guided tours provide a deeper understanding of the fort's strategic importance during the colonial era.

Cannons and Fortifications

Visitors can explore the fort's various cannons, buildings, and defensive structures, providing a glimpse into the island's military history.

Photographic Views

The elevated location of Fort King George offers panoramic views of Scarborough, the harbor, and the Caribbean Sea, making it a perfect spot for photography and capturing breathtaking vistas.

Botanical Gardens

Adjacent to Fort King George is the Tobago Botanical Gardens, showcasing a variety of tropical plants and flowers, adding to the beauty of the site.

Visiting Fort King George

Fort King George is situated in Scarborough, Tobago's capital, making it easily accessible for visitors staying in the town or other parts of the island.

Historical Tour

Visitors can explore the fort and its exhibits on their own, or join guided tours led by knowledgeable guides who provide historical context and information.

Scenic Views

The fort's location on a hilltop offers impressive views, and it's particularly picturesque during sunrise and sunset.

Little Tobago and Bird Sanctuary

Little Tobago, also known as Bird of Paradise Island, is a small and uninhabited island located off Tobago's northeastern coast. It is a protected area and a haven for birdwatchers, offering opportunities to spot various bird species in their natural habitat.

Key Features and Activities at Little Tobago and Bird Sanctuary

Birdwatching

Little Tobago is home to a variety of bird species, including the Red-billed Tropicbird, Frigatebirds, and the rare White-tailed Sabrewing hummingbird. Birdwatchers can observe these birds up close in their natural environment.

Guided Tours

Visitors must arrange guided tours to Little Tobago through authorized tour operators or guides. These tours usually include snorkeling or diving options, allowing visitors to explore the vibrant marine life around the island.

Snorkeling and Diving

The waters surrounding Little Tobago offer excellent snorkeling and diving opportunities, with opportunities to see coral reefs and marine life.

Nature Photography

The natural beauty of Little Tobago provides a fantastic backdrop for nature photographers, capturing unique bird species and breathtaking landscapes.

Visiting Little Tobago and Bird Sanctuary

Little Tobago is accessible via boat tours from the fishing village of Speyside in northeastern Tobago.

Guided Tours

Visitors must arrange guided tours to Little Tobago through authorized tour operators or guides. These tours often include snorkeling or diving options.

Birdwatching Preparation

Birdwatchers are advised to bring binoculars and remain quiet and respectful during birdwatching to avoid disturbing the birds.

Conservation Efforts

Little Tobago is a protected area, and visitors are expected to adhere to the guidelines and practices in place to preserve the island's ecological balance.

Englishman's Bay

Englishman's Bay is a pristine and secluded beach nestled along Tobago's northern coast. Its unspoiled beauty, calm waters, and lush green surroundings make it a favorite spot for nature lovers and those seeking tranquility.

Key Features and Activities at Englishman's Bay

Beach Relaxation

Englishman's Bay is less developed than some of Tobago's other beaches, making it an excellent choice for those seeking a serene and quiet beach experience. The calm and clear waters provide a beautiful environment for swimming and tanning.

Nature Walks

The beach is surrounded by lush rainforests and verdant hills, offering opportunities for nature walks and hiking. A short hike uphill from the beach provides stunning panoramic views of the coastline and the Caribbean Sea.

Picnicking

Englishman's Bay is an ideal spot for picnics. Many visitors bring their own food and drinks to enjoy a day of relaxation in a natural setting.

Turtle Watching

During nesting season (March to August), visitors may have the opportunity to witness leatherback and hawksbill turtles coming ashore to lay their eggs.

Visiting Englishman's Bay

Englishman's Bay is located on Tobago's northern coast, approximately 15 kilometers (about 9 miles) from the town of Castara and 18 kilometers (about 11 miles) from Scarborough.

Accessibility

While the beach is accessible by car or taxi, the final approach to the bay requires descending a steep and winding hill. Some visitors prefer to walk down to the beach from the main road, enjoying the natural beauty along the way.

Lack of Facilities

Englishman's Bay is relatively undeveloped, and there are limited facilities on the beach. Visitors are encouraged to bring their own supplies, including food, drinks, and sunscreen.

Main Ridge Forest Reserve

Main Ridge Forest Reserve is the oldest protected rainforest in the Western Hemisphere, covering over 3,000 hectares (about 7,400 acres) of land in Tobago. This ecologically diverse forest reserve is home to an array of flora and fauna, making it a must-visit destination for nature enthusiasts and hikers.

Key Features and Activities at Main Ridge Forest Reserve

Hiking Trails

Main Ridge Forest Reserve offers a network of well-maintained hiking trails that wind through the lush rainforest, providing opportunities to observe various plant and animal species.

Birdwatching

The reserve is a haven for birdwatchers, with opportunities to spot a wide variety of bird species, including parrots, motmots, and hummingbirds.

Wildlife Encounters

The forest reserve is home to various wildlife, including agoutis, armadillos, and opossums. Lucky visitors might catch a glimpse of these elusive creatures.

Waterfalls

Some of the hiking trails in Main Ridge Forest Reserve lead to picturesque waterfalls, such as Gilpin Trace and Twin River Falls. The cascading waters and natural pools create a refreshing retreat within the forest.

Visiting Main Ridge Forest Reserve

Main Ridge Forest Reserve is located in the interior of Tobago and can be accessed from various points, including the villages of Roxborough and Bloody Bay.

Guided Tours

For a more enriching experience, visitors are encouraged to join guided tours led by knowledgeable local guides who can provide insights into the forest's ecological importance.

Hiking Safety

Hiking in the rainforest requires proper footwear and insect repellent. It's essential to stay on marked trails and be mindful of the environment to minimize the impact on the delicate ecosystem.

Castara Bay

Castara Bay is a charming fishing village nestled along Tobago's northern coast. It offers a blend of picturesque beaches, friendly locals, and a vibrant fishing community.

Key Features and Activities at Castara Bay

Beaches

Castara Bay is blessed with two stunning beaches, Big Bay and Little Bay, both offering soft sand and clear waters. Big Bay is ideal for swimming and sunbathing, while Little Bay is known for its seclusion and calm waters, making it perfect for snorkeling and observing marine life.

Fishing

The village of Castara is home to a thriving fishing community, and visitors can witness the traditional art of fishing, as fishermen bring in their catch and prepare it for sale.

Local Culture

Castara offers a glimpse into Tobago's local culture, with opportunities to interact with friendly locals, sample traditional cuisine, and even participate in drumming sessions and cultural performances.

Sunset Views

Castara Bay is famous for its breathtaking sunsets. Visitors can enjoy stunning views of the sun setting over the Caribbean Sea, creating a magical and romantic atmosphere.

Visiting Castara Bay

Castara Bay is located on Tobago's northern coast, approximately 40 kilometers (about 25 miles) from Scarborough.

Accommodations

Castara Bay offers various accommodations, including guesthouses and beachfront resorts, allowing visitors to experience the village's authentic charm.

Local Cuisine

Several restaurants and eateries in Castara serve fresh seafood and traditional Tobagonian dishes, providing a taste of local flavors.

Nylon Pool

Nylon Pool is a shallow sandbar located in the middle of the sea, just off the southwestern coast of Tobago. Its clear and calm waters have earned it the nickname "Nylon Pool" due to its resemblance to a swimming pool.

Key Features and Activities at Nylon Pool:

Swimming

The nylon Pool is a popular spot for swimming, with its shallow and warm waters providing a safe and relaxing environment for all ages.

Healing Properties

It is believed that the waters of the Nylon Pool have rejuvenating and healing properties. Many visitors indulge in a refreshing swim, believing it will bring good luck and positive energy.

Boat Tours

Visitors can take boat tours to Nylon Pool, often combined with trips to Buccoo Reef for snorkeling. These tours provide insights into the island's marine life and ecosystems.

Visiting Nylon Pool

Nylon Pool is located off the coast of Pigeon Point Beach in Tobago's southwestern region.

Boat Tours

Boat tours to Nylon Pool can be arranged at Pigeon Point Beach or other tour operators in the area.

Swimming Safety

While swimming is safe at Nylon Pool, it's essential to remain cautious, especially during times of high tide or strong currents.

Fort Bennett

Fort Bennett is a historical site located on the southwestern coast of Tobago, offering stunning panoramic views of the Caribbean Sea and Pigeon Point.

Key Features and Activities at Fort Bennett:

Historical Site

Fort Bennett dates back to the 17th century and played a significant role in Tobago's history as a strategic military outpost.

Scenic Views

The fort's elevated location provides breathtaking views of the surrounding coastline, making it a popular spot for photography and enjoying the sunset.

Coastal Walks

The area around Fort Bennett offers opportunities for leisurely coastal walks, where visitors can enjoy the refreshing sea breeze and natural beauty.

Visiting Fort Bennett

Fort Bennett is located near Pigeon Point Beach and Crown Point in Tobago's southwestern region.

Accessibility

The fort is easily accessible by car, taxi, or even on foot for those staying in the nearby areas.

Speyside and Goat Island

Speyside is a quaint fishing village located on Tobago's northeastern coast, known for its relaxed atmosphere, beautiful beaches, and proximity to Goat Island. Goat Island, also known as Little Tobago, is a small uninhabited island just offshore from Speyside. Both destinations offer unique experiences for nature enthusiasts and birdwatchers.

Key Features and Activities at Speyside and Goat Island

Snorkeling and Diving

The waters around Speyside and Goat Island are teeming with marine life, making it a fantastic destination for snorkeling and diving. Coral reefs, colorful fish, and even the chance to spot manta rays and nurse sharks add excitement to underwater exploration.

Birdwatching at Goat Island

Goat Island is a designated bird sanctuary and a paradise for birdwatchers. The island is home to various seabird species, including red-billed tropicbirds, frigatebirds, and brown boobies. A visit to Goat Island offers a unique opportunity to observe these birds in their natural habitat.

Glass Bottom Boat Tours

For those who prefer to stay dry, glass bottom boat tours are available from Speyside, offering a glimpse into the underwater world without getting wet. These tours often include stops at Goat Island for birdwatching.

Speyside Waterfall

Speyside is also home to a picturesque waterfall, providing a refreshing oasis for visitors to enjoy amid the natural beauty of the area.

Visiting Speyside and Goat Island

Speyside is located on Tobago's northeastern coast, approximately 40 kilometers (about 25 miles) from Scarborough.

Boat Tours to Goat Island

Boat tours to Goat Island and the surrounding snorkeling and diving sites can be arranged at Speyside.

Birdwatching Tours

For a more specialized birdwatching experience at Goat Island, visitors can join guided birdwatching tours led by knowledgeable guides.

Tobago Cocoa Estate

Tobago Cocoa Estate offers a unique and immersive experience into the world of cocoa production, providing insights into the island's rich chocolate heritage.

Key Features and Activities at Tobago Cocoa Estate

Cocoa Plantations

Visitors can explore cocoa plantations and learn about the different varieties of cocoa trees and their cultivation processes.

Cocoa Harvesting and Processing

Witness the harvesting and processing of cocoa beans, from the pod to the drying and fermentation stages, which are critical for chocolate production.

Chocolate Making

Participate in chocolate-making workshops, where visitors can learn the art of crafting delicious chocolate treats and indulge in the flavors of locally produced chocolate.

Tasting Sessions

Enjoy guided chocolate tasting sessions, where you can savor the unique flavors of Tobago's artisanal chocolate.

Visiting Tobago Cocoa Estate:

Tobago Cocoa Estate is located in the Arnos Vale area on Tobago's southwestern coast.

Guided Tours

Visitors can join guided tours of the cocoa estate to fully appreciate the journey of cocoa from bean to bar.

Chocolate Souvenirs

The estate's shop offers a selection of locally made chocolate products and cocoa-related souvenirs to take home.

Chapter 8: Trinidadian Cuisine and Dining

Must-Try Local Dishes

Trinidadian cuisine is a delightful fusion of flavors influenced by various cultures, including African, Indian, Chinese, Spanish, and Middle Eastern. The country's rich culinary heritage has resulted in a diverse array of mouthwatering dishes that reflect the island's cultural diversity. From savory stews and spicy curries to delectable desserts, Trinidadian cuisine promises a unique and unforgettable gastronomic experience. In this section, we will explore some of the must-try local dishes that should be on every food enthusiast's list when visiting Trinidad.

Doubles

Doubles is one of Trinidad's most popular street foods, beloved by locals and visitors alike. It consists of two soft, fluffy bara (flatbreads) filled with a generous serving of curried channa (chickpeas). The dish is then topped with various chutneys, including tamarind and cucumber, and finished off with a sprinkle of spicy pepper sauce. Doubles are a staple for breakfast or as a quick and satisfying snack any time of the day.

Roti

Roti is a traditional Indian flatbread that has become an integral part of Trinidadian cuisine. It is typically served with a variety of delicious fillings, such as curry chicken, beef, or vegetables. The flaky, thin layers of the roti complement the rich and flavorful curries, creating a delightful combination. A popular version of roti is the dhalpuri roti, which has ground split peas mixed into the dough for added texture and taste.

Pelau

Pelau is a mouthwatering one-pot rice dish that reflects Trinidad's cultural diversity. It combines rice, pigeon peas, and a choice of meat (often chicken or beef), simmered in a flavorful blend of herbs, spices, and coconut milk. The dish takes on a beautiful caramel color as the rice cooks with the meat and seasonings. Pelau is often served with a side of coleslaw or a tangy pepper sauce.

Callaloo

Callaloo is a delicious and nutritious soup made from the tender leaves of the dasheen plant (taro), often cooked with crab or salted pork for added flavor. The leaves are simmered with okra, coconut milk, and various herbs and spices, resulting in a creamy and hearty soup with a distinctive earthy taste. Callaloo is typically served with a side of rice or roti.

Bake and Shark:

Bake and Shark is a quintessential Trinidadian beach food that has gained international fame. It consists of fried shark meat served between two pieces of fried bread, known as "bake." The sandwich is then topped with an array of condiments and sauces, including tamarind sauce, garlic sauce, and hot pepper sauce. The combination of crispy shark and soft bake, along with the flavorful toppings, creates an explosion of flavors and textures.

Crab and Dumplings

Crab and Dumplings is a traditional Trinbagonian dish that showcases the island's abundant seafood. The dish features fresh crab cooked in a rich tomato-based sauce with herbs and spices, served with tender dumplings made from flour and water. The dumplings soak up the delicious crab gravy, making every bite a burst of savory goodness.

Souse

Souse is a tangy and refreshing dish made with pickled pig's feet, chicken feet, or beef trotters. The meat is marinated in a mixture of lime or vinegar, water, onions, peppers, and other seasonings. It is usually served cold, making it a popular choice for hot days. Souse is often enjoyed with a side of avocado or cucumbers.

Buss-Up-Shut

Buss-Up-Shut, also known as "Paratha Roti," is a popular Trinidadian dish that consists of flaky and layered flatbread served with curried meats or vegetables. The name "Buss-Up-Shut" is derived from the way the roti is torn or "busted up" into pieces, resembling a torn-up shirt. The soft and buttery texture of the roti pairs perfectly with the flavorful curries, making it a favorite among locals and visitors alike.

Pastelles

Pastelles are a beloved Trinidadian dish typically enjoyed during the Christmas season. They are similar to tamales and consist of a cornmeal dough filled with a savory mixture of seasoned meat (usually pork or chicken) and olives, raisins, and capers. The filled dough is then wrapped in banana leaves and steamed to perfection, resulting in a delicious and aromatic treat with a unique blend of sweet and savory flavors.

Oil Down

Oil Down is a traditional dish from Trinidad and Tobago's sister island, Grenada, that has become popular across the entire country. It is a hearty one-pot meal made with breadfruit, salted meat (such as salted pork or codfish), vegetables, and coconut milk. The ingredients are simmered together, allowing the flavors to meld and creating a rich, comforting stew with a creamy coconut undertone.

KFC (Trinidad-style)

While you might be familiar with Kentucky Fried Chicken (KFC) in many parts of the world, Trinidad has its unique version of KFC that stands out from the rest. Trinidad-style KFC offers a blend of international flavors with a local twist. The menu includes not only the classic fried chicken but also unique additions like the "Doubles and a Piece" combo, which pairs KFC fried chicken with the popular local dish, Doubles.

Black Cake

Black Cake, also known as "Rum Cake," is a boozy and decadent dessert traditionally enjoyed during festive occasions, especially Christmas and weddings. The cake is made with a rich fruitcake base infused with rum and cherry brandy. The dried fruits, nuts, and spices used in the cake are soaked in alcohol for several weeks to create a flavorful and moist treat.

Popular Restaurants and Food Stalls

In Trinidad, you'll find an abundance of local eateries, food stalls, and restaurants that offer authentic and delicious Trinidadian cuisine. From bustling food markets to cozy family-run establishments, the culinary scene in Trinidad caters to all tastes and budgets. Here are some popular restaurants and food stalls that are renowned for their Trinidadian dishes:

Maracas Bay Bake & Shark (Maracas Bay)

Located at Maracas Bay, this iconic food stall is synonymous with the famous Bake and Shark dish. Their offerings of crispy fried shark served in warm bake with an array of flavorful toppings and sauces attract both locals and tourists. The beachside setting and mouthwatering flavors make it a must-visit spot for anyone exploring Trinidad's northern coast.

Chaud Creole (Woodbrook, Port of Spain)

Chaud Creole is a renowned restaurant in the heart of Port of Spain, offering a refined and contemporary take on traditional Trinidadian dishes. Their menu showcases a fusion of local and international flavors, with dishes like Crab and Callaloo Cannelloni and Jerk Duck with Cassava Dumplings. The elegant ambiance and creative culinary offerings make Chaud Creole a top choice for a special dining experience.

Ali's Roti Shop (San Juan)

Ali's Roti Shop is a popular spot for indulging in the mouthwatering flavors of Trinidadian roti. The menu features a variety of roti options, including Chicken, Goat, and Shrimp Roti, served with a side of delightful channa or dhal. This family-run establishment has earned a loyal following for its authentic and delicious roti creations.

Richard's Bake & Shark (Maracas Bay)

Another Bake and Shark hotspot at Maracas Bay, Richard's Bake & Shark is famous for its generous portions and flavorful combinations. The friendly staff and the option to customize your toppings make it a favorite among locals and visitors seeking a true Trinidadian culinary experience.

Doubles Man (Various Locations)

Doubles Man is a well-known mobile food stall that serves delicious doubles across multiple locations throughout Trinidad. Their freshly made bara and flavorful channa, complemented by various chutneys and pepper sauce, make it a convenient and tasty option for enjoying this classic Trinidadian street food.

Hott Shoppe (Various Locations)

Hott Shoppe is a chain of fast-food restaurants known for its signature Hott Roti Sandwiches, which feature a variety of fillings, including chicken, beef, and vegetables. Their delectable roti options and flavorful sauces make it a popular choice for a quick and satisfying meal.

Patraj Roti Shop (San Fernando)

Patraj Roti Shop in San Fernando is celebrated for its mouthwatering array of roti dishes, including Chicken, Beef, and Vegetable Roti. The traditional flavors and hearty portions keep patrons coming back for more.

Marabella Aunty Sally's (Marabella)

Marabella Aunty Sally's is a well-known spot for savoring the classic taste of Trinidadian cuisine. Their menu features local favorites such as Pelau, Curry Goat, and Stewed Chicken, all prepared with authentic flavors and love.

The Lighthouse Restaurant (Chaguaramas)

Situated in Chaguaramas, The Lighthouse Restaurant offers stunning waterfront views and a diverse menu that includes fresh seafood, local specialties, and international cuisine. It's an excellent spot to enjoy delicious food while taking in breathtaking sunset views.

Raps Chicken (Various Locations)

Raps Chicken is a popular fast-food chain in Trinidad, specializing in mouthwatering fried chicken and tasty sides. Their flavorful chicken options, coupled with a range of sauces and seasonings, make it a go-to choice for a quick and satisfying meal.

D' Original Curry Duck (Various Locations)

As the name suggests, D' Original Curry Duck is renowned for its deliciously spiced curry duck. Their flavorful duck dishes, served with rice and traditional sides, provide a taste of Trinidad's rich culinary heritage.

Buzo Osteria Italiana (Woodbrook, Port of Spain)

While not strictly Trinidadian, Buzo Osteria Italiana is famous for its authentic Italian cuisine and warm hospitality. The restaurant offers an extensive menu of classic Italian dishes, including pasta, pizza, and flavorful antipasti. It's a great option for those seeking a change of palate while still enjoying excellent dining in Trinidad.

The Waterfront Restaurant (Port of Spain)

Located on the waterfront in Port of Spain, this restaurant offers a picturesque setting and a diverse menu featuring local and international dishes. With an inviting ambiance and delicious cuisine, The Waterfront Restaurant is a popular choice for both locals and tourists.

Debe Doubles (Debe)

Debe Doubles is a well-known food stall in the town of Debe, offering authentic and flavorful doubles. The queues of eager customers waiting for their doubles are a testament to the stall's reputation for serving one of Trinidad's favorite street foods.

The Lighthouse Sports Bar & Grill (Chaguaramas)

Situated in Chaguaramas, The Lighthouse Sports Bar & Grill is a casual dining spot that offers a range of dishes, including tasty barbecued meats, local favorites, and classic pub fare. Its atmosphere and waterfront location make it a popular spot to unwind and enjoy good food.

Chapter 9: Shopping in Trinidad

Local Markets and Souvenirs

Trinidad offers a vibrant and diverse shopping experience, with an array of markets and shops where you can find everything from locally made handicrafts and unique souvenirs to fresh produce and authentic Trinidadian products. Whether you're looking for gifts to take back home or simply want to immerse yourself in the local culture, exploring the markets of Trinidad is a must. Here are some of the best local markets and souvenirs to explore:

Port of Spain Central Market

Port of Spain Central Market is the largest and most famous market in Trinidad, located in the heart of the capital city. This bustling market is a vibrant hub where locals and tourists alike come to shop for fresh produce, local delicacies, and a wide range of goods. The market is divided into various sections, each offering its unique products. You can find a variety of fruits, vegetables, spices, and condiments, as well as fresh seafood and meat. Additionally, the market has stalls selling local crafts, clothing, and souvenirs.

Key Features and Souvenirs

Local Crafts

Look for stalls selling traditional Trinidadian crafts, including handmade baskets, wood carvings, and pottery. These items are excellent souvenirs to take back home, representing the island's unique cultural heritage.

Local Foods

Taste and purchase authentic Trinidadian spices and condiments, such as curry powder, hot pepper sauces, and chutneys. These make for wonderful culinary souvenirs and can add a touch of Trinidadian flavor to your meals.

Local Snacks

Don't miss the opportunity to try local snacks like channa (roasted chickpeas), preserved fruits, and sweet treats like sugar cake and tamarind balls. These can be purchased as souvenirs or enjoyed as tasty snacks during your trip.

Chaguanas Market

Chaguanas Market is another popular market located in the bustling town of Chaguanas, about a 30-minute drive from Port of Spain. This vibrant market is known for its fresh produce, clothing, and local handicrafts. It is a great place to experience the lively atmosphere of a Trinidadian market and interact with friendly vendors.

Key Features and Souvenirs

Local Clothing

Chaguanas Market is a fantastic place to shop for local clothing, including colorful and comfortable Caribbean-style garments like tie-dye dresses, batik shirts, and beachwear.

Jewelry and Accessories

Look for stalls selling handmade jewelry and accessories, such as beaded necklaces, bracelets, and earrings, which make for beautiful and unique souvenirs.

San Fernando Market

San Fernando Market is located in the southern city of San Fernando and is the second-largest market in Trinidad. This bustling market is a lively hub where locals come to shop for fresh produce, spices, and household items. The market also features stalls selling a wide range of goods, including clothing, footwear, and souvenirs.

Key Features and Souvenirs

Spices and Herbs

San Fernando Market is an excellent place to purchase high-quality spices and herbs, such as saffron, cinnamon, and bay leaves. These aromatic ingredients can add a burst of flavor to your cooking and are perfect for souvenirs.

Local Handicrafts

Look for stalls selling unique handicrafts, such as handwoven rugs, embroidered tablecloths, and decorative wooden items. These locally made crafts make for meaningful and memorable souvenirs.

Queen's Park Savannah Craft Market

Queen's Park Savannah Craft Market is a popular shopping destination located near Queen's Park Savannah in Port of Spain. It is a dedicated craft market where you can find an extensive array of locally made handicrafts and souvenirs.

Key Features and Souvenirs

Art and Paintings

The craft market features stalls selling colorful paintings and artwork by local artists, showcasing the talent and creativity of Trinidad's artistic community.

Handmade Jewelry

Look for stalls selling handcrafted jewelry made from local materials like beads, shells, and natural stones. These unique pieces of jewelry make for eye-catching and meaningful souvenirs.

Cocobel Chocolates

For those with a sweet tooth, Cocobel Chocolates is a must-visit boutique chocolatier located in St. Ann's, Port of Spain. This artisanal chocolate shop produces high-quality chocolates made from Trinidadian cocoa beans.

Key Features and Souvenirs

Artisanal Chocolates

Cocobel Chocolates offers a wide selection of artisanal chocolates in various flavors, including dark, milk, and white chocolate infused with local ingredients like rum, coconut, and spices. These delectable chocolates are perfect for indulging in during your stay or as gifts to take back home.

Lara's Bay Local Craft Shop

Lara's Bay Local Craft Shop is located on the picturesque Maracas Beach and offers a charming selection of locally made crafts and souvenirs. It's a perfect stop after enjoying a day at the beach.

Key Features and Souvenirs

Shell Jewelry

The shop features a variety of shell jewelry, including necklaces, bracelets, and earrings, made from shells collected on the nearby beach. These pieces serve as beautiful reminders of your time spent in Trinidad.

Bamboo and Coconut Crafts

Look for handmade items crafted from bamboo and coconut, such as keychains, baskets, and decorative items. These eco-friendly souvenirs showcase the island's natural resources and creativity.

El Socorro Center for Wildlife Conservation

El Socorro Center for Wildlife Conservation is not just a market but also a social enterprise that supports wildlife conservation efforts in Trinidad. The center offers a unique shopping experience with a focus on sustainable products and local crafts.

Key Features and Souvenirs

Eco-Friendly Products

The center sells a range of eco-friendly products, including reusable bags, natural skincare products, and locally-made crafts that promote sustainable living.

Supporting Conservation

By purchasing souvenirs from this center, you contribute to wildlife conservation efforts in Trinidad, making your shopping experience more meaningful and impactful.

Please, note that when shopping in local markets and craft shops, don't forget to engage with the vendors and learn about the stories behind their products. Bargaining is not common in most established markets, but it may be acceptable in smaller craft shops. Additionally, ensure that you comply with customs regulations when purchasing souvenirs made from natural materials like shells and animal products.

Medulla Art Gallery

Medulla Art Gallery, situated in Woodbrook, is an alternative art space that embraces experimental and unconventional forms of art.

The gallery seeks to challenge traditional notions of art and encourages artists to push boundaries.

Key Features and Art Exhibitions

Multidisciplinary Art

Medulla Art Gallery hosts a diverse range of artistic expressions, including installations, performance art, video art, and interactive installations.

Experimental Projects

The gallery provides a platform for artists to explore experimental and innovative approaches to art, encouraging them to think beyond traditional art forms.

Horizons Art Gallery

With multiple locations across Trinidad, Horizons Art Gallery is a well-established art space that has been promoting local and Caribbean art for over 35 years. The gallery showcases a diverse collection of contemporary and traditional art pieces.

Key Features and Art Collection

Caribbean Artists

Horizons Art Gallery exhibits the works of talented Caribbean artists, reflecting the region's cultural richness and diversity.

Art Events and Workshops

The gallery hosts art-related events, including artist talks and workshops, fostering a sense of community and encouraging art appreciation.

Studio 66 Art Gallery

Studio 66 Art Gallery, located in Arima, is a contemporary art space that showcases the works of local and regional artists. The gallery's collection includes paintings, sculptures, and mixed media artworks.

Key Features and Art Exhibitions

Emerging Artists

Studio 66 Art Gallery provides a platform for emerging artists to exhibit their works, supporting their growth and development in the art world.

Community Engagement

The gallery actively engages with the local community through art-related events and initiatives, promoting the importance of art and culture in society.

Artie's Art Gallery

Artie's Art Gallery, situated in Chaguanas, offers a curated selection of art pieces and handicrafts by local artists and artisans. The gallery is known for its warm and welcoming atmosphere.

Key Features and Art Collection

Local Handicrafts

Artie's Art Gallery features a variety of locally made handicrafts, including sculptures, pottery, and handmade jewelry, representing the talent and creativity of Trinidad's artisans.

Affordable Art

The gallery offers a range of art pieces at different price points, making it accessible for visitors who want to purchase meaningful art without breaking the bank.

Please, note that art and craft galleries in Trinidad often rotate their exhibitions, so it's a good idea to check their schedules and current exhibits before planning your visit. Additionally, some galleries may charge an entrance fee, especially for special exhibitions and events.

Shopping Malls and Boutiques in Trinidad

Trinidad offers a diverse and exciting shopping experience, with an array of modern shopping malls and trendy boutiques scattered across the island. Whether you're looking for high-end fashion, unique souvenirs, or local designer pieces, Trinidad's shopping scene has something to cater to every taste and style. From bustling malls with international brands to charming boutiques with locally crafted items, here are some notable shopping destinations in Trinidad:

Trincity Mall

Trincity Mall, located in Trincity, just outside of Port of Spain, is one of the largest and most popular shopping centers in Trinidad. The mall features over 200 stores, including international brands, department stores, specialty shops, and dining options.

Key Features and Shopping Options:

Fashion and Apparel

Trincity Mall offers a wide selection of fashion and apparel stores, from well-known global brands to local boutiques. Visitors can find clothing for all ages and styles, including casual wear, formal attire, swimwear, and accessories.

Electronics and Technology

The mall is home to several electronics and technology stores, where you can shop for the latest gadgets, smartphones, laptops, and home appliances.

Entertainment

Trincity Mall includes an entertainment zone with a movie theater, arcade games, and activities for children, making it a great destination for family outings.

Westmall Shopping Centre

Westmall Shopping Centre, situated in Westmoorings, Port of Spain, is another popular shopping destination in Trinidad. The mall offers a mix of retail stores, dining options, and entertainment facilities.

Key Features and Shopping Options

Department Stores

Westmall hosts several department stores where shoppers can find a variety of products, including clothing, beauty products, home goods, and more.

Specialty Shops

The mall includes specialty shops selling items such as jewelry, accessories, books, and gifts, providing a unique and diverse shopping experience.

Food Court

Westmall's food court features a range of eateries serving local and international cuisine, making it a convenient spot for a meal or snack during your shopping trip.

Long Circular Mall

Long Circular Mall, located in St. James, Port of Spain, is a boutique-style shopping center with a focus on high-end fashion, accessories, and beauty products.

Key Features and Shopping Options

Designer Boutiques

Long Circular Mall is known for its designer boutiques, showcasing luxury brands and exclusive fashion collections.

Beauty and Cosmetics

The mall features beauty and cosmetics stores where visitors can shop for premium skincare products, makeup, and fragrances.

Upscale Dining

Long Circular Mall boasts a selection of upscale dining options, making it a perfect destination for a sophisticated lunch or dinner.

Gulf City Mall

Gulf City Mall, located in La Romain, San Fernando, is one of the largest shopping centers in southern Trinidad. It offers a mix of retail stores, restaurants, and entertainment venues.

Key Features and Shopping Options

Fashion and Accessories

Gulf City Mall hosts a variety of fashion stores catering to different tastes and budgets. Visitors can find clothing, footwear, and accessories for men, women, and children.

Home and Décor

The mall includes home and décor stores where shoppers can browse for furniture, household items, and decorative pieces.

Supermarkets

Gulf City Mall houses supermarkets and grocery stores, providing convenient shopping options for everyday necessities.

The Falls at Westmall

The Falls at Westmall, an extension of the Westmall Shopping Centre, is a premium shopping complex that caters to high-end shoppers and features a mix of luxury stores and upscale dining options.

Key Features and Shopping Options

Luxury Brands

The Falls at Westmall showcases luxury brands, including designer clothing, accessories, and high-end jewelry.

Fine Dining

The complex offers fine dining restaurants and cafes, providing a sophisticated culinary experience for shoppers and diners.

Ellerslie Plaza

Ellerslie Plaza, located in St. Clair, Port of Spain, is a well-established shopping center that has been serving the community for decades. It offers a mix of retail stores, services, and dining options.

Key Features and Shopping Options

Local Boutiques

Ellerslie Plaza features several locally owned boutiques where visitors can find unique clothing, accessories, and gifts created by Trinidadian designers.

Art and Craft Shops

The mall includes art and craft shops selling handmade items, such as paintings, sculptures, and decorative crafts, making it a great place to shop for authentic Trinidadian souvenirs.

Valsayn Shopping Plaza

Valsayn Shopping Plaza, located in Valsayn, is a charming shopping destination with a mix of stores and services catering to the local community.

Key Features and Shopping Options

Local Fashion and Beauty Stores

Valsayn Shopping Plaza is home to several local fashion boutiques and beauty stores, offering a selection of clothing, accessories, and cosmetics.

Restaurants and Cafes

The plaza includes restaurants and cafes where shoppers can enjoy a meal or refreshments during their visit.

UpMarket

UpMarket is a popular pop-up market that takes place on the last Saturday of every month at the Woodbrook Youth Facility in Port of Spain. It showcases a curated selection of local art, craft, fashion, and gourmet food products.

Key Features and Shopping Options

Local Art and Crafts

UpMarket provides a platform for local artisans and designers to showcase their unique creations, including handmade jewelry, art prints, home decor, and more.

Gourmet Food and Beverages

The market features a gourmet food section with vendors offering a variety of artisanal food products, such as organic produce, homemade desserts, and specialty beverages.

Chapter 10: Outdoor Activities and Adventures

Hiking and Nature Walks in Trinidad

Trinidad's natural beauty is a paradise for outdoor enthusiasts, with lush rainforests, cascading waterfalls, and picturesque trails waiting to be explored. Hiking and nature walks provide a fantastic way to immerse yourself in the island's diverse ecosystems, encounter unique flora and fauna, and experience breathtaking views. Whether you're an avid hiker or a leisurely nature enthusiast, Trinidad offers a range of trails suitable for all levels of fitness and experience. Here are some of the best hiking and nature walk destinations in Trinidad:

Asa Wright Nature Centre and Lodge

The Asa Wright Nature Centre and Lodge is a world-renowned bird-watching and eco-tourism destination located in the Northern Range of Trinidad. It offers a network of well-maintained trails that wind through the rainforest, providing visitors with an opportunity to spot a wide variety of bird species and other wildlife.

Hiking and Nature Walk Options

Discovery Trail

The Discovery Trail is a short and easy walk suitable for all ages and fitness levels. It offers a chance to observe colorful tropical birds, butterflies, and native plants.

Dunn's Trail

Dunn's Trail is a longer and more challenging hike that takes visitors deeper into the forest, providing a chance to spot rare and elusive bird species.

Avocat Waterfall and Three Pools

The Avocat Waterfall hike is a popular adventure located in southern Trinidad, near the village of Avocat. The trail leads to a stunning waterfall with three cascading pools, where hikers can take a refreshing dip in the crystal-clear waters.

Hiking and Nature Walk Options

Avocat Waterfall Trail

The trail is relatively short and moderately challenging, with some steep sections. It takes about 30-45 minutes to reach the waterfall, making it an ideal day trip for nature lovers.

Three Pools Hike

For more experienced hikers, there is an option to continue past the waterfall to explore the Three Pools area, which offers additional pools and beautiful natural scenery.

Paria Falls and Beach

The Paria Falls and Beach hike is one of the most iconic and picturesque adventures in Trinidad. The trail begins at the Blanchisseuse beach and takes hikers through the lush rainforest before arriving at the spectacular Paria Falls and secluded beach.

Hiking and Nature Walk Options

Paria Falls Hike

The hike to Paria Falls involves crossing several rivers and navigating through dense forests, which can be challenging but highly rewarding.

Paria Beach Hike

For a longer and more adventurous experience, hikers can continue past Paria Falls to reach the pristine Paria Beach, a remote and breathtakingly beautiful spot on Trinidad's northern coast.

Edith Falls and Bamboo Cathedral

Edith Falls and Bamboo Cathedral are two separate hiking experiences that can be combined into a thrilling adventure in the Northern Range of Trinidad.

Hiking and Nature Walk Options

Edith Falls Hike

The trail to Edith Falls offers a moderate hike through a dense forest, leading to a picturesque waterfall and natural pool. Hikers can take a refreshing swim in the cool waters.

Bamboo Cathedral Hike

The Bamboo Cathedral trail leads through a towering grove of bamboo trees, creating a magical and serene atmosphere. It's a short but enchanting hike suitable for all ages.

Matura River and Mermaid Pools

The Matura River and Mermaid Pools hike is an off-the-beaten-path adventure in eastern Trinidad, offering a unique experience in a beautiful and secluded natural setting.

Hiking and Nature Walk Options

Matura River Hike

The hike along the Matura River involves trekking through the riverbed, crossing small cascades, and admiring the surrounding rainforest.

Mermaid Pools Hike

For those seeking a more challenging adventure, continuing further upstream leads to the stunning Mermaid Pools, a series of cascading rock pools with clear blue waters.

Tamana Bat Caves and Gasparee Caves

The Tamana Bat Caves and Gasparee Caves are two distinct cave exploration experiences in Trinidad, perfect for adventure seekers and those interested in spelunking.

Hiking and Nature Walk Options

Tamana Bat Caves

The Tamana Bat Caves require a guided hike and exploration, as they are located in a remote and rugged area. Hikers can witness thousands of bats flying out of the caves at dusk, creating an awe-inspiring natural spectacle.

Gasparee Caves

The Gasparee Caves are accessible by a short boat ride from the mainland to Gasparee Island. Once there, visitors can explore the stunning limestone caves, stalactites, and subterranean chambers.

Water Sports and Diving in Trinidad

Trinidad's stunning coastline and crystal-clear waters offer a paradise for water sports enthusiasts and diving aficionados. Whether you seek adrenaline-pumping activities or serene underwater explorations, the island's marine treasures provide a diverse range of water-based adventures. From surfing and kayaking to scuba diving and snorkeling, Trinidad's aquatic playground is waiting to be explored. Here are some of the best water sports and diving experiences in Trinidad:

Surfing

Trinidad's northern and eastern coastlines are known for their excellent surfing conditions, attracting wave riders from near and far. The island's consistent swells and warm waters create an ideal environment for surfers of all levels to catch some waves.

Surfing Spots

Toco

The village of Toco, located on the northeastern tip of Trinidad, is a popular surfing destination. Its exposed coastline receives consistent Atlantic swells, making it a favorite spot for experienced surfers.

Las Cuevas

Las Cuevas Beach, on the northern coast, is a beginner-friendly surfing spot. The gentle waves and sandy bottom create a welcoming environment for those new to surfing.

Maracas Bay

Maracas Bay is not only famous for its beautiful beach but also for its surf breaks, attracting both locals and visitors seeking great waves.

Kayaking

Kayaking is a fantastic way to explore Trinidad's calm rivers, serene mangrove forests, and hidden coves. Whether you prefer a leisurely paddle or an adventurous journey, kayaking offers a unique perspective of the island's lush landscapes.

Kayaking Spots

Caroni Swamp

The Caroni Swamp, located in Central Trinidad, is a popular kayaking destination. Guided tours take visitors through winding waterways, offering opportunities to spot the national bird of Trinidad and Tobago, the scarlet ibis.

Nariva Swamp

The Nariva Swamp, on Trinidad's eastern coast, is another kayaking hotspot. The swamp's tranquil waters provide a peaceful and immersive experience in nature.

Matura River

The Matura River in eastern Trinidad offers a scenic kayaking adventure through the lush rainforest, with the opportunity to spot various bird species and other wildlife.

Scuba Diving

Trinidad's underwater world is a hidden treasure teeming with marine life, colorful coral reefs, and captivating shipwrecks. Scuba diving enthusiasts can explore a range of dive sites suitable for all levels, from beginners to experienced divers.

Scuba Diving Sites

Chacachacare Island

Located off Trinidad's northwestern coast, Chacachacare Island offers fascinating diving opportunities, including exploring the remains of a sunken navy frigate, the HMS Thetis.

Tobago Cays

While technically part of Tobago, not Trinidad, the Tobago Cays are easily accessible from the southern coast of Trinidad. These pristine diving sites boast vibrant coral reefs and abundant marine life, including turtles, rays, and sharks.

Snorkeling

For those who prefer to stay closer to the surface but still want to marvel at Trinidad's marine wonders, snorkeling is an excellent option. The island's reefs and protected bays provide excellent snorkeling opportunities for all ages.

Snorkeling Spots

Buccoo Reef

Although situated off the coast of Tobago, Buccoo Reef is accessible from Trinidad and offers one of the best snorkeling experiences in the region. This protected marine park boasts an array of coral formations and marine life.

Tyrico Bay

Tyrico Bay, located on Trinidad's north coast, is a popular snorkeling spot with clear waters and vibrant coral formations. Snorkelers can encounter tropical fish, colorful corals, and even sea turtles.

Gasparee Caves

The Gasparee Caves, accessible from Trinidad's western coast, offer a unique snorkeling experience in and around the limestone caves and rock formations.

Stand-Up Paddleboarding (SUP)

Stand-up paddleboarding is a relaxing and enjoyable way to explore Trinidad's calm coastal waters and scenic lagoons. It's also an excellent full-body workout that allows you to glide peacefully across the water.

SUP Spots

Caroni Bird Sanctuary

Paddleboarding through the mangrove-lined waterways of the Caroni Bird Sanctuary is a serene experience, providing the chance to spot various bird species and other wildlife.

Manzanilla Beach

The calm waters of Manzanilla Beach on Trinidad's eastern coast are ideal for beginners and those looking for a tranquil paddleboarding session.

Maracas Bay

Maracas Bay's picturesque setting makes it a popular spot for stand-up paddleboarding, where you can admire the beautiful shoreline from the water.

Jet Skiing

For those seeking a burst of adrenaline, jet skiing offers an exhilarating way to experience Trinidad's coastal beauty while zooming across the waves.

Jet Skiing Locations

Las Cuevas Beach

Las Cuevas Beach provides an excellent location for jet skiing, with its spacious sandy shores and inviting waters.

Maracas Bay

Maracas Bay's popular beach is another spot where visitors can rent jet skis for an exciting ride along the coastline.

Pigeon Point, Tobago

While Tobago is a separate island, Pigeon Point is easily accessible from Trinidad and offers fantastic jet skiing opportunities in its clear blue waters.

Bird Watching and Wildlife Tours in Trinidad

Trinidad's rich biodiversity and varied ecosystems make it a haven for bird watchers and wildlife enthusiasts. With over 470 bird species recorded on the island, including some rare and endemic ones, Trinidad offers unparalleled opportunities to spot and appreciate the diverse avian life. Additionally, the island's lush rainforests, swamps, and savannas are home to a wide range of other fascinating wildlife species. Whether you're a seasoned birder or a nature lover looking to immerse yourself in Trinidad's natural wonders, bird watching and wildlife tours are an incredible way to connect with the island's fauna. Here are some of the best bird-watching and wildlife tour experiences in Trinidad:

Caroni Bird Sanctuary

The Caroni Bird Sanctuary is a must-visit destination for bird watching in Trinidad. Located in the Caroni Swamp, this protected area is home to one of the world's most spectacular birding sights—the nightly flight of scarlet ibises returning to roost.

Bird Watching and Wildlife Tours

Scarlet Ibis Boat Tours

Guided boat tours take visitors through the mangrove-lined waterways of the Caroni Swamp at dusk, offering an unforgettable opportunity to witness thousands of scarlet ibises flying in formation to their nesting sites. Other bird species, including herons, egrets, and kingfishers, can also be spotted during the tour.

Wildlife Encounters

Besides the scarlet ibis, the Caroni Bird Sanctuary is home to numerous other bird species, such as tricolored herons, snowy egrets, and various raptors. Additionally, visitors may have a chance to see caimans, snakes, and other wildlife during the tour.

Asa Wright Nature Centre and Lodge

The Asa Wright Nature Centre and Lodge, nestled in the Northern Range, is a renowned bird-watching and ecotourism destination. The center's lush surroundings and well-maintained trails provide excellent opportunities for birders to spot a wide variety of species.

Bird Watching and Wildlife Tours

Guided Birding Tours

Experienced naturalist guides lead birding tours through the rainforest trails of the Asa Wright Nature Centre, pointing out various bird species and sharing fascinating insights about their behaviors and habitats.

Verandah Viewing

The center's open-air verandah serves as a popular bird-watching spot, where visitors can relax and observe a range of birds, including toucans, tanagers, and hummingbirds, as they visit nearby feeding stations.

Nariva Swamp

The Nariva Swamp, located on Trinidad's eastern coast, is a significant wetland area with diverse habitats, making it an excellent destination for bird watching and wildlife tours.

Bird Watching and Wildlife Tours

Boat Tours

Guided boat tours through the waterways of the Nariva Swamp provide opportunities to spot various bird species, including herons, ibises, and the secretive limpkin. Additionally, the swamp is home to howler monkeys and caimans.

Matura River Tours

The Matura River, which flows through the Nariva Swamp, is another birding hot spot. Boat tours along the river offer encounters with waterfowl, raptors, and various migratory birds.

Yerette Hummingbird Sanctuary

The Yerette Hummingbird Sanctuary, located in Maracas Valley, is a private residence turned bird sanctuary that specializes in attracting and observing hummingbirds up close.

Bird Watching Tours

Hummingbird Viewing

Visitors can sit on the verandah of the sanctuary and observe a dazzling array of hummingbirds, including the blue-chinned sapphire, copper-rumped hummingbird, and white-necked jacobin, as they visit specially designed feeders.

Guided Tours

The sanctuary offers guided tours led by the owners, Theo and Gloria Ferguson, who are passionate about hummingbirds and provide fascinating insights into their behavior and biology.

Asa Wright's Oilbird Cave Tour

Asa Wright Nature Centre also offers an exclusive tour of the Oilbird Cave, where visitors can witness the unique and rare oilbirds in their natural habitat.

Oilbird Cave Tour

Guided Excursion

Visitors embark on a guided hike to a secluded cave, where oilbirds roost during the day. Guides provide detailed information about the behavior and ecology of these fascinating nocturnal birds.

Little Tobago Island

Although Little Tobago Island is technically part of Tobago, it's easily accessible from the northeastern coast of Trinidad and offers excellent bird-watching opportunities.

Bird Watching Tours

Bird Island Boat Tours

Guided boat tours take visitors to Little Tobago Island, where they can encounter nesting colonies of magnificent frigatebirds, red-billed tropicbirds, and brown boobies.

Glass-Bottom Boat Tours

Some boat tours feature glass-bottom boats, allowing visitors to observe the vibrant marine life beneath the waves as they make their way to Little Tobago Island.

Chapter 11: Traveling with Pets to Trinidad

For pet owners planning to visit Trinidad, traveling with their furry companions can be a rewarding experience. However, it's essential to be well-prepared and aware of the necessary procedures and requirements to ensure a smooth and stress-free journey for both you and your pets. Here's a comprehensive guide on traveling with pets to Trinidad:

Research Pet Regulations and Requirements

Before making any travel arrangements, research the pet import regulations and requirements of Trinidad and Tobago. The country has specific rules and restrictions regarding the importation of pets to prevent the spread of diseases and ensure the safety of both animals and humans.

Pet Import Requirements

- Import Permit: You will need to obtain an import permit from the Veterinary Services Division of the Ministry of Agriculture, Land, and Fisheries in Trinidad. The application should be made well in advance of your travel date.
- Rabies Vaccination: Ensure that your pet is up-to-date on its rabies vaccination. Pets must have received the vaccine at least 30 days before entering Trinidad, but not more than 12 months before travel.

- Health Certificate: Obtain a health certificate issued by a licensed veterinarian within seven days of travel. The certificate should state that your pet is healthy and free from any contagious diseases.
- Microchip: Some countries may require your pet to be microchipped for identification purposes. Check if this is a requirement for Trinidad.
- Quarantine: There is no mandatory quarantine for pets entering Trinidad from many countries. However, pets traveling from certain high-risk regions may be subject to quarantine upon arrival.

Choose Pet-Friendly Airlines

When traveling by air, choose airlines that have pet-friendly policies and amenities for traveling with pets. Each airline has its specific rules and guidelines regarding pet transportation, so it's crucial to inquire about their pet policies before booking your flight.

Considerations for Air Travel with Pets

- Pet Size and Weight Restrictions: Different airlines have varying size and weight limits for pets traveling in the cabin or cargo hold. Ensure that your pet meets the airline's requirements.
- Pet Carrier: Your pet will need an airline-approved pet carrier that provides enough space for your pet to stand, turn around, and lie down comfortably.
- Booking in Advance: Airlines often have limited space for pets in the cabin, so book your pet's ticket well in advance to secure a spot.
- Health Certificate: Most airlines require a recent health certificate issued by a veterinarian, confirming your pet's good health and fitness to travel.

- Direct Flights: Whenever possible, opt for direct flights to minimize stress and travel time for your pet.

Pet-Friendly Accommodation

When choosing accommodation for your stay in Trinidad, look for pet-friendly hotels, guesthouses, or vacation rentals that welcome pets. Many hotels and accommodations have specific pet policies and may charge additional fees for pets.

Pet-Friendly Accommodation Tips

- Advance Booking: Inform the accommodation about your pet during the booking process to ensure they have pet-friendly rooms available.
- Pet Policies: Inquire about the specific pet policies, including any size or breed restrictions and additional fees.
- Pet Amenities: Some pet-friendly accommodations may offer pet amenities, such as pet beds or food/water bowls, to enhance your pet's comfort.
- Pet Exercise Areas: Choose accommodations with nearby parks or walking areas where you can take your pet for exercise and bathroom breaks.

Pet-Friendly Transportation within Trinidad

Once in Trinidad, you'll need to navigate the island with your pet. While public transportation may not allow pets, there are other options available for getting around with your furry friend.

Rental Cars

Renting a car is a convenient option for pet owners as it allows you to have control over your pet's comfort and safety during transportation.

Pet Taxis

Some taxi services in Trinidad are pet-friendly and allow well-behaved pets to travel with their owners. Always confirm with the taxi service before booking.

Pet-Friendly Tours and Activities

When participating in tours and activities on the island, inquire if they allow pets to join or if they can recommend pet-friendly options.

Pet Safety and Comfort

During your travels, it's essential to prioritize your pet's safety and comfort. Traveling can be stressful for animals, so take steps to ensure your pet's well-being throughout the journey.

Pet Travel Essentials

- Pet Carrier: Use a well-ventilated and secure pet carrier for air travel or car rides. Familiarize your pet with the carrier before the trip to make them feel more comfortable.
- Identification Tags: Ensure your pet wears a collar with up-to-date identification tags, including your contact information.
- Water and Food: Bring enough water and pet food for the journey, and keep your pet hydrated and fed during layovers and breaks.
- Comfort Items: Pack familiar toys, blankets, or bedding to provide a sense of comfort and security for your pet.
- Regular Breaks: During road trips or layovers, take regular breaks to allow your pet to stretch, exercise, and use the bathroom.

Please, note that it is crucial to begin the planning process for traveling with your pet well in advance of your trip to Trinidad. Each step, from obtaining the necessary permits to arranging pet-friendly accommodations and transportation, requires careful attention to ensure a successful journey for both you and your beloved pet.

Chapter 12: Safety and Health Tips

Emergency Contacts

When traveling to Trinidad, being prepared for emergencies is essential to ensure your safety and well-being. Familiarize yourself with emergency contacts and healthcare facilities on the island to receive prompt assistance if needed. Here are some important emergency contacts in Trinidad:

Emergency Services

Police: 999
• In case of any criminal activity, accidents, or emergencies requiring immediate police assistance, dial 999 for emergency services.
Ambulance and Fire: 990
• For medical emergencies or fire-related incidents, call 990 to request an ambulance or fire service.

Hospitals and Medical Facilities

Port of Spain General Hospital
Address: Charlotte St, Port of Spain, Trinidad
• Contact: +1 868-623-2951
Eric Williams Medical Sciences Complex
Address: Uriah Butler Hwy, Mount Hope, Trinidad
• Contact: +1 868-645-2640
San Fernando General Hospital
Address: Independence Ave, San Fernando, Trinidad

- Contact: +1 868-652-3581

Sangre Grande Hospital
Address: Eastern Main Rd, Sangre Grande, Trinidad
- Contact: +1 868-668-2461

Scarborough General Hospital (Tobago)
Address: Fort St, Scarborough, Tobago
- Contact: +1 868-639-2551

British High Commission
Address: 19 St Clair Ave, St Clair, Port of Spain, Trinidad
- Contact: +1 868-225-7270

Canadian High Commission
Address: 3-3A Sweet Briar Rd, St Clair, Port of Spain, Trinidad
- Contact: +1 868-622-6232

Tourism Police

Tourism Police Unit (Trinidad and Tobago Police Service)
The Tourism Police Unit assists tourists and visitors with safety and security concerns. They are available to provide information and support during your stay.
- Contact: +1 868-624-4006

7. Coast Guard:
Trinidad and Tobago Coast Guard
For emergencies at sea or maritime-related incidents, contact the Coast Guard.
- Contact: +1 868-634-4444

Health Precautions and Vaccinations

Prioritizing your health and well-being while traveling to Trinidad is crucial to ensure a safe and enjoyable trip. Here are some health precautions and vaccination recommendations to consider before your journey:

Routine Vaccinations

Ensure that your routine vaccinations are up-to-date before traveling to Trinidad. These may include vaccinations for measles, mumps, rubella, diphtheria, tetanus, pertussis, influenza, and varicella (chickenpox).

Hepatitis A and B

Hepatitis A and B are viral infections that can be transmitted through contaminated food, water, or contact with infected individuals. It's recommended to get vaccinated for both hepatitis A and B, especially if you plan to explore local cuisine and have interactions with the local population.

Yellow Fever

Trinidad is not currently listed as a country with a risk of yellow fever transmission. However, if you are traveling from a country with a yellow fever risk, you may be required to show proof of yellow fever vaccination upon entry to Trinidad.

Mosquito-Borne Diseases

Trinidad is a tropical destination, and mosquito-borne illnesses, such as dengue fever, chikungunya, and Zika virus, can be a concern. Take precautions to avoid mosquito bites, such as using insect repellents, wearing long-sleeved clothing and pants, and staying in accommodations with screened windows.

Sun Safety

Trinidad's sunny climate makes sun safety essential. Protect yourself from sunburn and potential heatstroke by wearing sunscreen with a high SPF, using sunglasses and a wide-brimmed hat, and staying hydrated.

Safe Food and Water Practices

To avoid foodborne illnesses, follow safe food and water practices:
- Drink Bottled Water: Stick to bottled water and avoid tap water, especially in rural areas.
- Eat Cooked Food: Opt for freshly cooked and hot meals, and avoid consuming raw or undercooked food.
- Peel Fruits and Vegetables: When enjoying local fruits and vegetables, wash and peel them to reduce the risk of contamination.
- Avoid Street Food: While tempting, be cautious with street food, and choose vendors with good hygiene practices.

Travel Health Insurance

Consider purchasing travel health insurance that covers medical emergencies, hospitalizations, and medical evacuations. It provides peace of mind in case of unexpected health issues during your trip.

Prescription Medications

Make sure you have enough prescription medication for the duration of your trip. Carry them in their original containers with clear labels, and bring a copy of your prescriptions in case they are needed.

Seek Medical Advice

Before traveling, consult your healthcare provider or a travel medicine specialist to discuss any specific health concerns related to your trip to Trinidad. They can provide personalized recommendations based on your health history and itinerary.

Emergency Medication Kit

Pack a small emergency medication kit with essentials like pain relievers, antihistamines, anti-diarrheal medication, adhesive bandages, and any medications prescribed by your doctor.

Chapter13: Cultural Etiquette and Tips for Travelers

Respectful Behavior and Customs

When visiting Trinidad, understanding and respecting the local customs and cultural norms is essential to ensure positive interactions and to show appreciation for the country's rich heritage. Trinidad is a diverse and multicultural nation with a blend of African, Indian, European, and indigenous influences, which have shaped its unique customs and traditions. Here are some key cultural etiquette tips to keep in mind during your visit:

Greetings and Politeness

• Warm Greetings: Trinidadians are known for their warm and friendly nature. Greet people with a smile and a friendly "hello" or "good morning" when meeting someone for the first time or entering a shop or establishment.
• Handshakes: Handshakes are common for greetings, especially in formal settings. Offer a firm handshake, and maintain eye contact as a sign of respect.
• Use of Titles: Address people using their titles, such as "Mr.," "Mrs.," "Miss," or "Doctor," followed by their last name. If unsure about how to address someone, it's acceptable to ask politely.

Language and Dialect

• English: English is the official language of Trinidad and is widely spoken and understood. Communication should not be a barrier for English-speaking travelers.
• Local Dialect: Trinidad's unique dialect is a fusion of various cultural influences, including English, African, Hindi, and Spanish. While most Trinidadians speak English, learning a few basic greetings and phrases in the local dialect can be appreciated and may help you connect with locals on a deeper level.

Personal Space and Physical Contact

• Respect Personal Space: Trinidadians generally value personal space, so avoid standing too close or invading someone's bubble during conversations.
• Physical Contact: While handshakes are common, avoid hugging or kissing someone you have just met unless they initiate the gesture.

Cultural Sensitivity

• Religious Sites: When visiting religious sites or attending religious events, dress modestly and remove shoes when required. Show respect for religious practices and customs.
• Taboos and Superstitions: Be sensitive to local taboos and superstitions. For example, it is considered disrespectful to point at people with your finger or foot.

Tipping Etiquette

• Restaurants and Services: Tipping is customary in Trinidad. In restaurants, a service charge may already be included in the bill, but an additional tip of 10-15% is appreciated for good service. Similarly, tipping taxi drivers and hotel staff is common.

Respect for Nature and Environment

• Eco-Tourism Practices: Trinidad is known for its stunning natural beauty and biodiversity. Practice eco-friendly tourism by not disturbing wildlife, avoiding littering, and following designated trails in protected areas.

Photography Etiquette

• Ask for Permission: Before taking photos of locals or in private settings, it's polite to ask for their permission. Some people may not feel comfortable being captured in photographs.

Understanding Local Traditions

Trinidad's rich cultural tapestry is woven with a diverse array of traditions and celebrations that reflect its multi-ethnic heritage. Embracing and understanding these traditions will deepen your appreciation for the local culture. Here are some key traditional customs and celebrations in Trinidad:

Carnival

- The Greatest Show on Earth: Carnival is Trinidad's most famous and vibrant cultural event. Held annually in the days leading up to Ash Wednesday, it is a dazzling spectacle of color, music, dance, and revelry. The festivities include masquerade bands, calypso competitions, steelpan music, and the famous J'ouvert street party.
- Costumes: Carnival costumes are elaborate and meticulously designed. They often feature intricate beadwork, feathers, and sequins, reflecting the creativity and craftsmanship of local artists.
- Panorama: The National Steelband Panorama Competition showcases the musical prowess of steelpan bands, a Trinidadian invention that has become a symbol of the nation's culture.

- Clay Lamps: During Divali, houses are adorned with clay lamps (diyas), candles, and colorful decorations. Fireworks and the lighting of lamps create a breathtaking spectacle.

Eid-ul-Fitr and Eid-ul-Adha

- Islamic Festivals: Eid-ul-Fitr marks the end of Ramadan, the Islamic holy month of fasting, and is celebrated with communal prayers, feasting, and giving of gifts.
- Eid-ul-Adha: Also known as the Festival of Sacrifice, Eid-ul-Adha commemorates the willingness of Prophet Ibrahim to sacrifice his son, Isma'il. It involves prayers, the sacrifice of animals, and the distribution of meat to the needy.

Hosay Festival

- Religious Procession: Hosay is a Shia Muslim festival that commemorates the martyrdom of the Prophet Muhammad's grandsons, Imam Hassan and Imam Hussain. It features ornate tadjahs (replicas of tombs) carried in a colorful and vibrant procession.

Phagwa (Holi):

- Festival of Colors: Phagwa, or Holi, is a Hindu spring festival celebrated with the throwing of colored powders and water, symbolizing the triumph of good over evil.

Christmas and Parang

- Festive Celebrations: Christmas is widely celebrated in Trinidad, with decorations, caroling, and religious services. The traditional Parang music, with Spanish influence, is a hallmark of the Christmas season.

Folklore and Folk Music

- Steelpan Music: The steelpan, often referred to as the steel drum, is the national instrument of Trinidad and Tobago. It originated from recycled oil drums and has since become an integral part of the country's musical heritage.
- Calypso and Soca: Calypso and soca music are deeply rooted in Trinidad's culture. Calypso is known for its social commentary, while soca is a more upbeat and dance-oriented genre often associated with Carnival.

Cuisine

- Diverse Flavors: Trinidad's cuisine is a delectable fusion of influences from various cultures, including African, Indian, Spanish, and Creole. Traditional dishes like roti, doubles, callaloo, and pelau offer a taste of the island's diverse culinary heritage.

Art and Craftwork

- Local Artisans: Trinidad is home to talented artisans who create beautiful handicrafts, pottery, and wood carvings. Visiting local craft markets and galleries allows you to admire and purchase these unique creations.

Family and Community

- Strong Sense of Community: Trinidadian culture places significant importance on family and community ties. Respect for elders and a strong sense of community cohesion are integral aspects of the local culture.

Note that Trinidad's culture is a colorful mosaic of traditions, customs, and celebrations, each contributing to the island's vibrant identity. By embracing and respecting these customs and traditions, you can create meaningful connections with the local population, enrich your travel experience, and gain a deeper appreciation for the beauty of Trinidadian culture.

Chapter 14: Language and Useful Phrases

Language plays a significant role in cultural exchange and communication during travel. In Trinidad, English is the official language, making it easy for English-speaking travelers to navigate their way around the island. However, Trinidad's unique cultural blend has also influenced the development of a distinct local dialect known as Trinidadian English or Trinidadian Creole. Understanding some common phrases and expressions in the local dialect can enhance your interactions with locals and make your travel experience even more enriching. Here are some essential language tips and useful phrases to help you communicate effectively during your trip to Trinidad:

Official Language

English

English is the official language of Trinidad and is widely spoken and understood. It is the language used in government, education, media, and formal settings. Most Trinidadians are bilingual, proficient in both English and the local dialect.

Trinidadian English (Trinidadian Creole)

Trinidadian English, also known as Trinidadian Creole or simply "Trini," is a unique and colorful dialect that reflects the island's diverse cultural heritage. It incorporates elements of English, African languages, Hindi, Spanish, and other influences. While most Trinidadians are fluent in standard English, they may also switch to the local dialect in informal settings or during casual conversations. Here are some common phrases in Trinidadian English:

Greetings and Expressions

- Wah gwan?: "What's going on?" or "What's up?"
- Ahight: "Alright" or "Okay."
- Lime: To "lime" means to hang out or socialize with friends.
- Bacchanal: Drama or a commotion, often used to describe a noisy argument or dispute.
- Boof: To "boof" someone means to insult or criticize them.
- Maco: Someone who is nosy or always prying into other people's business is called a "maco."
- Stupes: A sound made by sucking one's teeth, usually in response to annoyance or irritation.
- Broughtupsy: Refers to someone with good manners and proper upbringing.

Food and Cuisine

- Doubles: A popular Trinidadian street food made of fried flatbread filled with curried chickpeas.
- Roti: A delicious wrap made of Indian flatbread filled with various savory ingredients like curry chicken, curry goat, or channa (chickpeas).
- Pelau: A flavorful one-pot dish made with rice, meat (usually chicken or beef), and pigeon peas, cooked in coconut milk and seasoned with local herbs and spices.
- Callaloo: A traditional Trinidadian soup or stew made from the leaves of the dasheen plant, often combined with crab or other seafood.

- Bake and Shark: A popular beachside dish consisting of deep-fried shark meat served in fried dough (bake) with various condiments and toppings.

Expressions of Affection and Friendship

- Breds / Bredren: Slang term for friends or buddies, derived from the word "brethren."
- Famalay: A term used to refer to close friends or a tight-knit group, similar to the word "family."
- Luv: An affectionate way of addressing someone, similar to "love."
- Darling: A term of endearment used for friends or loved ones, regardless of gender.

Directions and Travel

- De Savannah: Refers to the Queen's Park Savannah, a large open park in Port of Spain, the capital city.
- Maxi Taxi: A shared, large-capacity minibus used for public transportation across the island.
- Zess: To "zess" means to have fun or party, often used to describe a lively social gathering or event.
- Broughtupsy: Refers to someone with good manners and proper upbringing.

Essential Phrases in Trinidadian English

- Hello: "Hello" is widely understood in Trinidad as a standard greeting.
- Good morning: "Good morning" is the appropriate greeting during the morning hours.
- Good afternoon: "Good afternoon" is used as a greeting during the afternoon hours.
- Good evening: "Good evening" is the standard greeting in the evening.

- Thank you: In Trinidadian English, you can also say "tank yuh" or "thanks."
- Please: "Please" is expressed as "pleez" in Trinidadian English.
- Excuse me: To get someone's attention or to apologize for a minor inconvenience, you can say "excuse me" or "s'cuse me."
- Where is...?: To ask for directions, say "Where is...?" followed by the name of the place you're trying to find. For example, "Where is the beach?"
- How much is this?: If you're shopping or inquiring about the price of something, say "How much is this?"
- Yes: "Yes" is the same as in standard English, but in Trinidadian English, it may be pronounced as "yeah" or "yea."
- No: "No" is the same as in standard English.
- I don't understand: If you're having difficulty understanding something, say "I don't understand" or "I eh understand" in Trinidadian English.
- I'm sorry: To apologize, you can say "I'm sorry" or "I sorry."

Please, note that Trinidadian English is a delightful and expressive dialect that reflects the island's vibrant culture and history. While English remains the primary language for official and formal communication, embracing some commonly used expressions in Trinidadian English can lead to more engaging and enjoyable interactions with locals. Don't be afraid to use these phrases during your travels and immerse yourself in the colorful language of Trinidad.

As your time in Trinidad comes to a close, you may find yourself feeling a mixture of emotions. The island's warm hospitality, stunning landscapes, vibrant culture, and delicious cuisine have left an indelible mark on your heart. Saying goodbye to Trinidad may not be easy, but the memories and experiences you have gained will stay with you forever.

Printed in Great Britain
by Amazon